Religion and Culture in the Renaissance and Reformation

Habent sua fata libelli

Volume XI
of
Sixteenth Century Essays & Studies
Charles G. Nauert, Jr., General Editor

ISBN: 0-940474-11-5

Composed by Paula Presley, NMSU, Kirksville, Missouri
Cover Design by Teresa Wheeler, NMSU Designer
Printed by Edwards Brothers, Ann Arbor, Michigan
Text is set in Bembo II 10/12

Religion and Culture

in the
Renaissance and Reformation

Steven Ozment
Editor

Volume XI
Sixteenth Century Essays & Studies

Library of Congress Cataloging-in-Publication Data

Religion and culture in the Renaissance and Reformation.

(Sixteenth century essays & studies ; v. 11)
Papers from a symposium held at Harvard University, November 1987.
Includes index.
1. Religion and culture--Europe--History--Congresses. 2. Renaissance--Congresses. 3. Reformation--Congresses. I. Ozment, Steven E. II. Series.
BL65.C8R443   1989   274'.05   89-11446
ISBN 0-940474-11-5 (alk. paper)

The woodcuts on pages 63 and 120 are printed by permission of Hacker Art Books, Inc. from Max Geisberg, *The German Single-Leaf Woodcut: 1500-1550,* rev. and ed. Walter L. Strauss, New York, 1974. The woodcut on pages 24 and 78 is printed by permission of Abaris Books, Inc., from Walter L. Strauss, ed., *The German Single-Leaf Woodcut 1550-1600,* New York: 1975, vol. 3, pp. 1292, 1362.

This book has been brought to publication with the
generous support of
Northeast Missouri State University

Table of Contents

General Editor's Introduction

This collection of papers from a symposium held in November 1987 at Harvard University demonstrates clearly, as Steven Ozment indicates in his introductory essay, that even scholars approaching the history of the Renaissance and Reformation from the perspective of popular culture cannot avoid making religion a central topic of their work. Although the symposium was intended to deal, and did in fact deal, with urban communities, the principal point of connection among the papers turned out to be the role of religion in the cultural life of the people rather than the role of urban society. The volume offers several fresh perspectives on the interaction between religion and the life of the people – principally but not exclusively urban people – in the period.

Charles G. Nauert, Jr.
General Editor
Sixteenth Century Essays and Studies

Introduction

ON NOVEMBER 5 AND 6, 1987, historians gathered at Harvard University to hear and discuss papers on the topic, "Cities and Their Cultures in the Renaissance and Reformation." Three generations of historians were present. The papers arranged themselves around three themes: Civic Culture, Learned Culture, and Popular Culture. A slight bias toward German history could be detected.

To a remarkable degree, religion emerged as the unifying theme of the conference, far more than either "cities" or "culture." There may be several explanations for this. The enormous popularity of the term "culture" among historians today has tended to render it more a code word for research that aspires to be *au courant* than a category of any precise historical meaning. "Cities," too, is a rather broad, vague, and overworked category. That religion should, to such a degree, provide access to these large topics reflects the prominence and richness of the religious history of the Renaissance and Reformation. That historians of such varying persuasions should locate and illumine dominant historical forces of the age primarily through a discussion of religion also attests to a major historiographical development in the last two decades.

Civic Culture

An area of considerable interest in recent historiography has been rituals, collective human action on a grand scale. There is much recorded history without any conscious contemporary comment on its meaning or importance to those involved. Aided by modern anthropology and sociology, historians have attempted to treat such events as "texts" in their own right, as legitimate as, and perhaps even more revealing than, written texts. Thomas A. Brady, Jr., sees this as a valuable approach and decries the comparative neglect of such studies in German historiography. He illustrates some of the possibilities it holds with concise case studies of two ceremonial entries by alien ruling authorities into German towns. The first is the 1507 entry of Bishop William, count of Honstein, into inhospitable Strasbourg. As this event unfolds, it becomes clear to the reader that the city viewed the bishop as a rival whose authority it was disinclined to recognize. The second, far grander entry is that of Emperor Charles V into more receptive, but also still very cautious, Augsburg in 1530. By looking carefully at the order of greeting, the personnel involved, the routes taken, the stops made, Brady discovers important aspects of the city's self-perception, its attitude toward imperial authority, even the forces at work behind future political decisions.

Nowhere was the manipulation of space for political purposes more sophisticated than in the cities of Renaissance Italy. Those in power used traditional symbols and rituals to promote a sense of security within and

3

fidelity to the status quo, and hence to enhance their own authority and control over the populace. Dissenters and rebels, to the contrary, sought to legitimate themselves and to justify radical social change by use of such symbols and rituals. As Edward Muir makes clear, the less centralized and controlled a city's ritual space, the more likely one is to find a society in serious conflict. Muir shows how iconic sacred language reflected social divisions and political aspirations in four diverse Italian cities: Venice, where sacred space was to an unusual degree successfully dominated by ruling authority; Florence, whose sacred space, like its society, was often fragmented and readily manipulated by antagonistic social groups; Naples, with still deeper social divisions and more widely dispersed and competitive sacred centers; and, finally, comparatively tiny Udine, where conflict in society seemed most extreme and the symbols and rituals representing social aspirations had become largely secular and no longer religious.

Learned Culture

The study of the Reformation still awaits a Moses who can lead it through the sea of contemporary polemics between social and intellectual historians and into a historiography both mindful and tolerant of all the forces that shape historical experience. Heiko A. Oberman attempts to point the way by calling attention to the common ground between the *eruditi* and the *simplices* in the fifteenth-century lay/clerical reform movement known as the Modern Devotion. Obviously, in the past as in the present, both educated and uneducated people absorb and reflect the values of their larger societies. The Modern Devotion sought its recruits among ordinary laity, who, in turn, embraced the learning and culture they discovered within the brother and sister houses of the movement. The Modern Devotion thus became a community at once ordinary and elite, practical and intellectual, both anti-scholastic and respectful of learning. For Oberman, the movement represents in microcosm the intellectual and social context of the Reformation. It was, he argues, out of such integration of the worlds of the learned and the simple, almost a century old and extending beyond the communities of the brothers and the sisters, that the revolt of the Protestant pamphleteers came.

Most scholars would agree that in the 1520s and 1530s, particularly within the Empire, successful Protestant reforms shared common elements. They were led by local reform-minded clergy, who were respected by the laity. They were intellectual and literate, served by humanistic educational reforms and by the printing press. And they steadily gained the support of magistrates, who early, and often grudgingly, appreciated their political necessity, if not their religious desirability. Scholars have also recognized the limits to such generalizations, recognizing that each urban reform, occurring within a community with its own unique culture and politics, also had its distinctive features.

William J. Bouwsma calls attention to the numerous and striking ways in which the Reformation in Geneva, the most Protestant of cities, differed from that in Strasbourg and Basel, which adhered closely to the general pattern. How did Calvin, an alien minister in a city initially neither deeply interested in religious reform nor particularly well equipped to implement it, manage to take the Reformation farther than the more advantaged reformers of Strasbourg and Basel had done? Bouwsma believes the explanation lies in the political and cultural "backwardness" of Geneva, which made it possible for Calvin and his followers to create and control the instruments of reform to a degree not found elsewhere.

Popular Culture

For both learned men, like Martin Luther and Paracelsus, and the masses of Germany's ordinary people, the sixteenth century was a magical world, filled with spirits of assorted shapes and talents, a sizeable number of which were demonic. Among the learned, belief in such spirits seems only to have posited a smaller and less complex array of demons.

H. C. Erik Midelfort maintains that by the second half of the sixteenth century people everywhere in Germany had become convinced that their world was in the grip of the Devil. Belief in the Devil and in demonic possession had become especially well-established among ordinary people due largely to epidemic witchcraft trials, which also peaked in the second half of the century. For most theologians, demonic possession was to be explained as a punishment for sin. But in the published contemporary literature on the subject, numerous pious people, particularly young girls of absolutely impeccable reputation, had fallen under the Devil's spell and abjured the Christian faith with the most terrible consequences. Although actual examples of such possession are few and far between, they nonetheless attest a phenomenon very real in the minds of people at the time. On the one hand, they suggest a kind of creative laicization of learned speculation on the Devil and his work. On the other, some of these stories may have been contrived, or at least elaborated, by reigning shepherds of souls to keep credulous laity in line.

During the later Middle Ages, magic was popular in both rural and urban society and among both literate and illiterate people. Its popularity and gradual decline in the late sixteenth and seventeenth centuries have been documented by scholars over the last two decades. R. Po-chia Hsia looks at perhaps the most horrific example of alleged demonic magic: Jewish ritual murder of Christian children to obtain their blood for private use. On the one hand, such myths reveal the depth of Christian fear of a competitive Jewish culture; but they also became a basis for legal and political action against Jews in the later Middle Ages. Though very rare, trials of Jews for ritual murder of Christians are a vivid commentary on the anti-Semitism of late medieval and Reformation Europe.

Due in part to the enlightening impact of Luther's religious revolution, myths of demonic Jewish magic actually diminished by the late sixteenth century. But their content remained. Where they had once served as legal and political tools to contain and coerce Jews, such myths, kept alive as cultural artifacts, became vivid reminders for subsequent generations of Christians of Jewish perfidy and past criminal activity. The myths, as Hsia makes clear, left the courtroom only to find their place in the history books. Pogroms ended, but anti-Semitism gained a new lease on life.

These brief remarks only highlight and hardly do full justice to the richness of the essays that follow, which in fresh and provocative ways suggest the variety of research going on today in the religious and cultural history of the Renaissance and Reformation. At the Harvard conference, each pair of papers had a commentator. The comments of Natalie Zemon Davis on the papers of Professors Muir and Brady, and those of Eugene F. Rice, Jr., on the papers of Professors Oberman and Bouwsma, were not preserved; but the analysis of elite and popular culture presented by Gerald Strauss in his comments on the work of Professors Hsia and Midelfort appears as the concluding essay in this volume.

Steven Ozment

Harvard University
April 1989

I

Civic Culture

Rites of Autonomy, Rites of Dependence: South German Civic Culture in the Age of Renaissance and Reformation

Thomas A. Brady, Jr.[1]

IN RECENT DAYS, programs for a restoration of Western Civilization's values seem to bloom all around us. Restorationists want a return to the classic values of the West, an odd assortment of folk ranging from the ancient Greeks through the medieval English to what a dim-witted journalist recently described as "Japan and the other nations of the West." Genealogy, a genial wit once said, is a common social disease, and argument about historical paradigms often turns on the genealogies of ideas, values, and mentalities. In this respect, the restorationist program reminds one of Sir Boyle Roche, a member of the ill-fated Irish Parliament at the end of the eighteenth century. Sir Boyle complained of talk about our debt to posterity and asked, "Why should we do anything for posterity? What has posterity done for us?" He explained that by "posterity" he meant not our ancestors but those who came just after them.[2]

Arguments about ancestors marked the debates about the discipline of history during the 1960s, a decade much reviled by the restorationists. Then emerged powerful challenges to the idea of Western Civilization, which had itself arisen just before 1900 as a pedagogy suited to America's newly sensed world/historical mission.[3] The idea claimed, as William H. McNeill has written, "affiliation with a tradition of Western civilization that ran back through modern and medieval Europe to the ancient Greeks and Hebrews."[4] This vision came to be challenged by one that holds that "the American way of life is no more than one variation among many to which humanity adheres."[5] The challenge opened history's stage to social classes, religious groups, peoples, and a whole gender, which had formerly hovered in the wings; it created, too, a need for ways to study people who had written little or nothing and who were, in Eric Wolf's words, "peoples without history."[6]

---

[1]This study is dedicated to the memory of Eric Cochrane – teacher, mentor, friend.

[2]Henry Boylan, *A Dictionary of Irish Biography* (New York: Barnes & Noble, 1978), 311-12.

[3]This was the time when the first modern history textbooks for public schools were being produced. Frances FitzGerald, *America Revised: History Schoolbooks in the Twentieth Century* (Boston: Little, Brown, 1979), 48-52.

[4]William H. McNeill, "Mythistory," in his *Mythistory and Other Essays* (Chicago: University of Chicago Press, 1986), 10.

[5]William H. McNeill, "The Care and Repair of Public Myth," in his *Mythistory and Other Essays,* 39.

[6]Eric R. Wolf, *Europe and the People Without History* (Berkeley: University of California Press, 1982), esp. 3-7.

No subject has benefited more from this change than has religion, conceived not only as "values" but also as lived ways of life. Fifteen years ago, religion was still a problematic enough subject to evoke from Eugene Genovese the comment that "in this secular, not to say cynical, age, few tasks present greater difficulty than that of compelling the well educated to take religious matters seriously."[7] Religion had not been absent from the idea of Western Civilization, which had, though over the objections of militant Hellenizers,[8] to admit religion chiefly in an idealized, synthetic form known as "Judeo-Christian values." Religions as ways of life, however, appeared at best as preparatory to, at worst as barriers to, the inevitable triumph of one of modernity's principal ingredients: secularization. Although change comes to the historical discipline at a pace much like that of the mills of God, eventually lived religion crept into even the most zealously modernist textbooks.[9]

At the heart of the new respect for religion as a way of life, rather than as ideas or "values" only, lay a new appreciation for ritual. The new attitude doubtless originated partly from reflections on the movements that swept American campuses during the later 1960s, when many young Americans demonstrated through collective words, signs, and deeds their determination to rescue their world from Western Civilization.[10] The palpable power of ritual actions and signs frightened many scholars, but it led others, among them historians, to at least three important insights. First, ritual – collective actions which created, conveyed, challenged, or interpreted the meanings of public and private life and linked the cosmic and the mundane worlds – structured the lives of Europe's common people.[11] Second, ritual structure shaped all popular culture, including politics, not just religious ceremonies

[7]Eugene Genovese, *Roll, Jordan, Roll: The World the Slaves Made* (New York: Random House, 1972), 161.

[8]See George G. Iggers, *The German Conception of History: The National Tradition of Historical Thought from Herder to the Present*, rev. ed. (Middletown, Conn.: Wesleyan University Press, 1983), 248-50.

[9]Such as R. R. Palmer and Joel Colton's *A History of the Modern World*, first published in 1950 and now in its 6th ed. (New York: Knopf, 1983).

[10]Observers who could see deeper than the "international insurrectionary style" noted the movement's love for the elements of song, accent, and dress associated with the people most despised by the American elites, the uplanders of the Upper South. To recognize such sounds in the voice of the movement's bard, Bob Dylan, a Jewish boy from Hibbing, Minnesota, is to see how profound this association became.

[11]Bob [= R. W.] Scribner, "Cosmic Order and Daily Life: Sacred and Secular in Pre-Industrial German Society," in Kaspar von Greyerz, ed. *Religion and Society in Early Modern Europe, 1500-1800* (London: Allen & Unwin, 1984), 17-32

strictu sensu.[12] Third, ritual conveyed meaning to whole societies and did not serve the interests of elites alone.[13]

Once identified, ritual could be recognized in many areas of life, including politics, where ritual came to offer a new gateway to the study of the mentalities of whole societies and parts of societies, especially urban ones, in early modern Europe. Soon, ritual actions – strikes in Lyon, confraternities in Florence, civic processions in Venice, and royal entries in France – became everywhere a stock-in-trade of the historians of European civic culture. Everywhere, that is, except among historians of the German-speaking cities.[14]

(1)

The late Eric Cochrane used to say that historians of Germany march to a different tune, and his view gains substance from the meager attention given to ritual by social historians of early modern Germany. The strongest case for the importance of religious ritual to German social history has been made not by a German-speaker but by an Australian, Bob Scribner, while the case for political ritual remains to be made. On the subject of ceremonial entries, for example, which provided Renaissance Europe's most spectacular form of political theater, there is an especially sophisticated literature on Italian[15] and French[16] entries, but little on the German-speaking world.[17]

This study aims not to suggest that Renaissance Germany's neglected civic pageantry may have rivaled that of Italy, which Bonner Mitchell has described as "probably the richest of the Renaissance, and certainly among

[12]Natalie Z. Davis, "From 'Popular Religion' to Religious Cultures," in Steven Ozment, ed., *Reformation Europe: A Guide to Research* (St. Louis: Center for Reformation Research, 1982), 321-41.

[13]R. W. Scribner, "Ritual and Popular Religion in Catholic Germany at the Time of the Reformation," *Journal of Ecclesiastical History* 35 (1984): 47-77.

[14]The lack does not reflect a paucity of information. Although a great deal is known about a related area of ritual, the Imperial Diets, it has not been exploited in this way. See Rosemarie Aulinger, *Das Bild des Reichstages im 16. Jahrhundert*, Schriftenreihe der Historischen Kommission bei der Bayerischen Akademie der Wissenschaften, no. 18 (Göttingen: Vandenhoeck & Ruprecht, 1980).

[15]Bonner Mitchell, *Italian Civic Pageantry in the High Renaissance: A Descriptive Bibliography of Triumphal Entries and Selected Other Festivals for State Occasions,* Biblioteca di bibliografia italiana, vol. 89 (Florence: Olschki, 1979); idem, *The Majesty of the State: Triumphal Progresses of Foreign Sovereigns in Renaissance Italy (1494-1600)* (Florence: Olschki, 1986).

[16]Bernard Guénée and Françoise Lehoux, eds., *Les entrées royales françaises de 1328 à 1515,* Sources d'histoire médiévale, vol. 5 (Paris: CNRS, 1968), 7-30; *Les Fêtes de la Renaissance,* ed. Jean Jacquot, 3 vols. (Paris: CNRS; 1956-75); Lawrence M. Bryant, *The King and the City in the Parisian Royal Entry Ceremony: Politics, Ritual, and Art in the Renaissance,* Travaux d'Humanisme et Renaissance, no. 216 (Geneva: Droz, 1986).

[17]What little there is, such as Karl Schlemmer, *Gottesdienst und Frömmigkeit in der Reichsstadt Nürnberg am Vorabend der Reformation* (Würzburg: Echter Verlag, 1980), 263-65, is rarely social in its approach.

the richest of all recorded history,"[18] or that of France, which Lawrence M. Bryant says "tended to describe the essence of national kingship in such a way as to exalt civic virtues and to encourage the preservation of urban liberties."[19] Yet the German cities, and especially the free cities,[20] did create elaborate traditions of civic pageantry, some examples of which may suggest how the study of political rituals might help us to understand German civic culture in the age of Renaissance and Reformation.

Civic culture's principal message taught the burgher that he and his fellows stood before God and the world as one body, the health of which (*bonum commune, gemeiner Nutz*) depended on their common devotion to unity, peace, justice, and the promotion of God's honor.[21] This civic gospel of the common good bombarded the burghers from all sides through official ideology, popular myth, and oppositional visions.[22] Nuremberg magistrates used it to justify a new law code in 1478;[23] Strasbourg's great cathedral preacher, John Geiler of Kaysersberg (d. 1510), taught that "We here . . . are all one body, and you and I are the members";[24] and voices of the "communal reformation,"[25] which culminated in the German Peasants' War, demanded a society based on peace, justice, brotherhood, and the Christian common good.[26] Of course, official voices called upon tradition, while oppositional voices called upon the Bible and the "godly law."[27] They

[18]Mitchell, *Majesty of State*, 3.

[19]Bryant, *The King and the City*, 22.

[20]On the definition of free cities, see Thomas A. Brady, Jr., *Turning Swiss: Cities and Empire, 1450-1500*, Cambridge Studies in Early Modern History (Cambridge: Cambridge University Press, 1985), 9-15.

[21]See the seminal essay by Hans-Christoph Rublack, "Grundwerte in der Reichsstadt im Spätmittelalter und in der frühen Neuzeit," in Horst Brunner, ed., *Literatur in der Stadt: Bedingungen und Beispiele städtischer Literatur des 15. bis 17. Jahrhunderts*, Göppinger Arbeiten zur Germanistik, 343 (Göppingen: Kümmerle, 1982), 9-36. (English: "Political and Social Norms in Urban Communities in the Holy Roman Empire," in Peter Blickle, Winfried Schulze, and Hans-Christoph Rublack, *Religion, Politics and Social Protest: Three Studies on Early Modern Germany*, ed. Kaspar von Greyerz [London: Allen & Unwin, 1984], 24-60.)

[22]Edward Muir employs this distinction. See his *Civic Ritual in Renaissance Venice* (Princeton: Princeton University Press, 1981), 57.

[23]Quoted in Rublack, "Political and Social Norms," 26 n. 8.

[24]Quoted from his *Brösamlein,* ed. Johannes Pauli (Strasbourg: Johannes Grüninger, 1517), in Brady, *Turning Swiss*, 122.

[25]Peter Blickle, *Gemeindereformation: Die Menschen des 16. Jahrhunderts auf dem Weg zum Heil* (Munich: Oldenbourg, 1986). The thesis was already formulated in Blickle's *Die Reformation im Reich*, Uni-Taschenbücher, no. 1181 (Stuttgart: Eugen Ulmer Verlag, 1982).

[26]Peter Blickle, *The Revolution of 1525: The German Peasants' War from a New Perspective*, trans. Thomas A. Brady, Jr., and H.C. Erik Midelfort (Baltimore: Johns Hopkins University Press, 1981), 87-93.

[27]See Heiko A. Oberman, *Masters of the Reformation: The Emergence of a New Intellectual Climate in Europe*, trans. Denis Martin (Cambridge: Cambridge University Press, 1981), 280-94.

nevertheless shared a language and a corporate metaphor and a belief in the political, moral, and even religious self-sufficiency of the commune.[28]

Some writers have taken this language of corporate metaphor to be the heart of civic culture,[29] and many civic rituals do confirm this identification. On certain days, for example, the commune went to church not as an amorphous "laity," but as a commune, especially on Corpus Christi, the greatest communal religious feast.[30] At Nuremberg on that day, the two parishes paraded through the streets, led by their priests and rose-crowned magistrates; at Strasbourg the magistrates appeared *in corpore,* flanked by the guilds and the clergy, and marched from church to church through the city.[31] Through such rites of autonomy,[32] the burghers as communal church and as sacral commune acted out their corporate autonomy before God and the world.

The greatest rite of civic autonomy was Schwörtag, when the commune installed new magistrates and the burghers swore to uphold the law and to obey the magistrates.[33] At Lucerne, for example, where magistrates were elected twice a year, the burghers swore the old oath:

> The commune swears to foster the good and honor of our city, to keep it from harm, to uphold the city's laws, liberties, and customs and to obey the charter, as it has come down to us, and to obey the magistrates.[34]

[28]On corporatist thought, see Antony Black, *Guilds and Civil Society in European Political Thought from the Twelfth Century to the Present* (Ithaca: Cornell University Press, 1984).

[29]See my critique of Bernd Moeller, in Thomas A. Brady, Jr., *Ruling Class, Regime and Reformation at Strassburg, 1520-1555,* Studies in Medieval and Reformation Thought, no. 22 (Leiden: Brill, 1978), 3-7; and again in idem, "The 'Social History of the Reformation' between 'Romantic Idealism' and 'Sociologism': A Reply," in Wolfgang J. Mommsen, Peter Alter, and Robert W. Scribner, eds., *The Urban Classes, the Nobility and the Reformation: Studies on the Social History of the Reformation in England and Germany,* Publications of the German Historical Institute, London, vol. 5 (Stuttgart: Klett-Cottta Verlag, 1979), 40-43. A very much stronger, theoretically well supported case for viewing the free city as a social organism is made by Erdmann Weyrauch, *Konfessionelle Krise und soziale Stabilität: Das Interim in Strassburg 1548-1562,* Spätmittelalter und Frühe Neuzeit. Tübinger Beiträge zur Geschichtsforschung, 7 (Stuttgart: Klett-Cotta, 1978), which is grounded in the idealist sociology of Niklaus Luhmann. See my review of this very interesting and neglected study in *The Catholic Historical Review* 67 (1981): 134-35.

[30]In Venice, according to Muir, *Civic Ritual,* 223, Corpus Christi was "the consummate annual procession by land."

[31]Schlemmer, *Gottesdienst und Frömmigkeit in der Reichsstadt Nürnberg,* 263-65; Luzian Pfleger, *Kirchengeschichte der Stadt Strassburg im Mittelalter,* Forschungen zur Kirchengeschichte des Elsass, vol. 6 (Colmar: Alsatia Verlag, 1941), 201-2.

[32]Sometimes such ceremonies commemorated civic rather than ecclesiastical feasts. At Strasbourg, for example, four annual Masses at the civic altar (Stadtaltar) in Strasbourg's cathedral commemorated the victories over the Burgundians in the 1470s. Pfleger, *Kirchengeschichte der Stadt Strassburg,* 198-99.

[33]Wilhelm Ebel, *Der Bürgereid als Geltungsgrund und Gestaltungsprinzip des deutschen mittelalterlichen Stadtrechts* (Weimar: Hermann Böhlaus Nachfolger, 1958), 23-37.

[34]Ibid., 24.

Such rites often found, as each January at Strasbourg, the magistrates high on a scaffold before the principal church or the town hall, where all could see them, and where they stood like captains on the quarterdeck of a ship, the city, manned by its crew, the burghers. Here, before God and the world, massed patricians and guilds spoke the old words in a civil counterpart to the feast of Corpus Christi.

Rites of autonomy, therefore, confirmed the ideology and the myth of the communal autonomy. The South German cities also acted out rites of dependence, which displayed the forces, both internal and external, that threatened the political, moral, and religious self-sufficiency of the communal status quo. Such were the "rites of violence,"[35] a rich tradition of German urban riots that stretched from the first guild revolts in the fourteenth century to the Reformation era and beyond.[36] In the early Reformation era emerged another rite of violence, the iconoclastic riot.[37] In the "war against the idols," the iconoclasts of the Reformation era elevated ritual violence to what Carlos Eire has called "one of the most important tactics in the process of religious change in some communities."[38] It did not replace, however, the traditional violent confrontation between magistrates and people, such as the Schilling affair at Augsburg in early August 1524, which began as a popular defense

[35]The term comes from Natalie Zemon Davis, "The Rites of Violence: Religious Riot in Sixteenth-Century France," *Past and Present* 59 (May 1973); reprinted in her *Society and Culture in Early Modern France. Eight Essays* (Stanford: Stanford University Press, 1975), 152-88.

[36]See Rhiman A. Rotz, "'Social Struggles' or the Price of Power? German Urban Uprisings in the Late Middle Ages," *Archiv für Reformationsgeschichte* 76 (1985): 64-95; Christopher R. Friedrichs, "Citizens or Subjects: Urban Conflict in Early Modern Germany," in Miriam U. Chrisman and Otto Gründler, eds., *Social Groups and Religious Ideas in the Sixteenth Century*, Studies in Medieval Culture, vol. 13 (Kalamazoo: Medieval Institute, 1978), 46-58, 164-69; idem, "Urban Conflicts and the Imperial Constitution in Seventeenth-Century Germany," *Journal of Modern History* 58, Supplement (December 1986): S98-S123. Both writers emphasize the continuity of pattern through the Reformation era.

[37]The first years of the sixteenth century witnessed a sharp increase in urban disturbances in South Germany, as they did in Italy. See Erich Maschke, "Deutsche Städte am Ausgang des Mittelalters," in his *Städte und Menschen: Beiträge zur Geschichte der Stadt, der Wirtschaft und Gesellschaft 1959-1977* (Beiheft 68 der *Vierteljahrschrift für Sozial- und Wirtschaftsgeschichte*; Wiesbaden: Franz Steiner Verlag, 1980), 56-99, esp. 75-76, 95, n. 206; Lauro Martines, *Power and Imagination: City-States in Renaissance Italy* (New York: Random House, 1979), 295-96.

[38]Carlos M. N. Eire, *War Against the Idols: The Reformation of Worship from Erasmus to Calvin* (Cambridge: Cambridge University Press, 1986), 106. Eire has put the subject on an entirely new footing, though on the German cities Carl C. Christensen's *Art and the Reformation in Germany* (Athens: Ohio University Press; Detroit: Wayne State University Press, 1979), 13-41, 66-109, is still useful. See also Lionel Rothkrug, "Holy Shrines, Religious Dissonance and Satan in the Origins of the German Reformation," *Historical Reflections / Réflexions historiques* 14 (1987): 143-286, esp. 187-89.

of a Franciscan preacher and ended in the judicial murders of two old weavers.[39]

Such "rites of violence" were rites of dependence in two senses, because they challenged the adequacy of official civic ritual, and because they briefly opened political life to persons – journeymen, working women, the poor and the marginals[40] – who normally possessed no voice, even though the city depended on their labor and services. The mingling of such folk with the burghers in the uncontrolled drama of mass protest served notice on magistrates and burghers of an ominous weakness in the gospel of civic autonomy.

Besides the dramas of unrest, South German civic culture contained other rites of dependence, which revealed the existence and nature of the powers who ruled the extramural world. The burghers did not rule this world, though their livelihoods depended on it. I want to describe two examples of one of the most important of such rites, the entry, to show how the study of political theater might help the historians of civic culture in the German-speaking world.

(2)

Sebastian Brant (ca. 1457-1521),[41] Strasbourg's town clerk and author of *The Ship of Fools*, recorded in great detail the entry of Bishop William,

---

[39]The most detailed account is still Friederich Roth, *Augsburgs Reformationsgeschichte 1517-1530*, 4 vols. (Munich: Theodor Ackermann, 1901-11) 1:156-70; and there are some interesting details in Götz Freiherr von Pölnitz, *Jakob Fugger: Kaiser, Kirche und Kapital in der oberdeutschen Renaissance*, 2 vols. (Tübingen: Mohr [Paul Siebeck], 1949-51), 1:571-73.

[40]Knut Schulz, *Handwerksgesellen und Lohnarbeiter: Untersuchungen zur oberrheinischen und oberdeutschen Stadtgeschichte des 14. bis 17. Jahrhundert* (Sigmaringen: Jan Thorbecke Verlag, 1985); Merry Wiesner, *Working Women in Renaissance Germany* (New Brunswick, N.J.: Rutgers University Press, 1986); Franz Irsigler and Arnold Lassotta, *Bettler, Gaukler, Dirnen u. Henker: Randgruppen und Aussenseiter in Köln 1300-1600* (Cologne: Greven Verlag, 1984).

[41]We sorely need a full study of Brant. The biographical details are most readily available in Edwin H. Zeydel, *Sebastian Brant* (New York: Twayne, 1967), chaps. 1-2. The conventional interpretation of Brant as a chaotic and moralistic writer and an uncritically conservative upholder of the status quo in church and state is given by Richard Newald, "Sebastian Brant," in Richard Newald, *Elsässische Charakterköpfe aus dem Zeitalter des Humanismus* (Colmar: Alsatia Verlag, 1944), 85-110, reprinted in Newald's *Probleme und Gestalten des deutschen Humanismus*, ed. Hans-Gert Roloff (Berlin: de Gruyter, 1963); and little is added by William Gilbert, "Sebastian Brant, Conservative Humanist," *Archive for Reformation History* 46 (1955): 145-67. This view has endured for more than a century, but there are now signs of a change. See Georg Baschnagel, *"Narrenschiff" und "Lob der Torheit": Zusammenhänge und Beziehungen*, Europäische Hochschulschriften, series 1, vol. 283 (Frankfurt/Main: Peter Lang, 1979), 7-47; Dieter Mertens, "Maximilian I. und das Elsass," in Otto Herding and Robert Stupperich, eds. *Der Humanismus in ihrer Umwelt*, Mitteilungen der Kommission für Humanismusforschung, no. 3 (Boppard: Harald Boldt Verlag, 1976), 177-200, in lieu of his still unpublished Freiburg Habilitationsschrift.

Count of Honstein, into his cathedral city on October 4, 1507.[42] William proved to be full of surprises. A warrior by training, he was soon ordained and said his first Mass, which his predecessor but one had not done during thirty-eight years in office.[43] Stranger yet, William came to be consecrated in Strasbourg's cathedral on Laetare Sunday 1507 and said Mass there on Corpus Christi 1508, things no bishop had done since the middle of the fourteenth century.[44] A sensational event interrupted his consecration, when King Maximilian and his entourage appeared unannounced to honor William and perhaps to show that the new ship was an Austrian client. William had risen through the patronage of Maximilian's chief antagonist, Elector Berthold of Mainz, who had died during the Bavarian War of 1504. In that war, Maximilian had crushed the expansionist dreams of the Elector Palatine, head of the House of Wittelsbach, and established Austria as the major power on the Upper Rhine.[45]

The prince-bishop of Strasbourg enjoyed preeminence in the whole land between the Vosges Mountains and the Black Forest, and from below Colmar to beyond Hagenau, but, like most Rhenish bishops, he could not reside in his cathedral city. He now came from his palace at Saverne, at the foot of the Vosges, to Strasbourg, where he arrived on October 4, 1507, at the Cronenbourg Gate on the city's northwestern edge. There he and his entourage were met by a civic escort – four leading magistrates, backed by sixty mounted and armored patricians – who had been cooling their heels for hours. The city into which they rode was packed with armed men, all burghers and rural subjects, for Strasbourg had not yet joined the rush to hire mercenary infantry (*Landsknechte*), which Maximilian and his advisers had initiated more than twenty years ago.[46] On the previous evening, more than five hundred armed peasants marched from villages in the civic territory into the city and stacked arms in three guildhalls for the night. "Many were very pleased," Brant writes,

> that these loyal folk had come so far on such short notice, that they
> arrived so well armed and ready for action, and that they were so

---

[42]On William's episcopate, see Francis Rapp, *Réformes et Réformation à Strasbourg: Église et société dans le diocèse de Strasbourg (1450-1525)*, Collection de l'Institut des Hautes études alsaciennes, no. 23 (Paris: Éditions Ophrys, 1975), 371-93.

[43]Robert of Bavaria was bishop from 1440 to 1478. See ibid., 321-45.

[44] Brant, "Bischoff Wilhelm," 296.

[45]See Brady, *Turning Swiss*, 72-79.

[46]Still definitive is Martin Nell, *Die Landsknechte: Entstehung der ersten deutschen Infanterie*, Historische Studien, vol. 123 (Berlin: E. Ebering, 1914); there are some new perspectives in Reinhard Baumann, *Das Söldnerwesen im 16. Jahrhundert im bayerischen und süddeutschen Beispiel: Eine gesellschaftsgeschichtliche Untersuchung*, Miscellanea Bavarica Monacensia, vol. 79 (Munich: R. Wölfle, 1978), 43-47.

loyal and obedient, so that the city of Strasbourg could justly regard them with all the more affection and trust.[47]

In fact, their ranks probably contained veterans of the Bundschuh rebellion of 1493 and future participants in the Bundschuh of 1517 and the great Peasants' War of 1525. Now, however, they joined more than fifteen hundred men from nineteen of the twenty guilds, who were armed, Brant says, "with good poleaxes, long pikes, or guns." The bishop, by contrast, was forbidden to bring infantry into the city.

The magistrates' stage directions for William's entry channelled his cavalcade along a route from the Cronenbourg Gate across the northern part of the city into its old heart and to the cathedral, the only place in Strasbourg where the bishop was still master. They stationed 2,071 armed burghers and peasants in six bands, each with a cannon and civic banner, at the points at which horsemen might try to veer from this narrow corridor into other parts of the city. As they rode along the Tanner's Ditch, the guests saw nothing of the city's political heart except the back side of the treasury, for every bridge southward was blocked by armed men.

Strasbourg, normally a city of twenty thousand souls, was this morning stuffed with visitors seeking a spectacle.

> All the houses and their windows were stuffed with people. Every street was filled with them walking or standing about, for an uncountable number of country folk from all around came to town early that morning in order to see this grand entry.[48]

Ahead, unbeknownst to Bishop William, the clergy surged out from the cathedral into the streets to meet him, as if to reclaim, for a moment, the city for its bishop.

At the broad Horse Market, where the cavalcade turned southward toward the cathedral, it met the city's true rulers. Warriors confronted warriors. On one side stood the bishop's mounted and armored officers and servitors, led by the marshal, Count Philip of Hanau, and the grand bailiff, Count Reinhard of Bitsch. Opposite them sat the mayor's party, 140 armored and mounted men in single rank with upright lances braced on saddles.[49] William, dressed in a white choir robe and black mantle, made a strikingly peaceful impression among all these armored men. The mayor's party doffed their headgear to honor William, but when he put his black beret back on, they covered again. To the peals of all the bells of Strasbourg's many churches, William's party now turned southward toward the cathedral,

---

[47]Brant, "Bischoff Wilhelm," 279.

[48]Ibid., 285.

[49]Thomas A. Brady, Jr., *Ruling Class, Regime and Reformation at Strasbourg, 1520-1555,* Studies in Medieval and Reformation Thought, vol. 22 (Leiden: Brill, 1978), 86, 362-72.

where he dismounted, donned his robes, and with miter and crozier entered the diocese's principal church to the great organ's strains of "Come, Holy Ghost."

William of Honstein entered his cathedral's choir as pastor and priest, though the burghers, who jammed their way into the church, could not see him at all. In those days, the three soaring Gothic naves – the burghers' church – were still divided from the dark Romanesque choir – the bishop's church – by a great stone rood screen. Atop this screen stood the civic magistrates and other notables, and they alone could see both the bishop and the priests in the choir and the burghers in the naves below. Their own preacher, John Geiler, was supposed to preach from his great Gothic pulpit, which was a gift of the commune; instead, after the Gospel the Mass rushed on to its end. William hurried away without giving the blessing.

Now disaster followed on disaster. William had invited the magistrates to dinner, and ceremonial dining "in the German manner" often meant six or seven hours at table.[50] At William's table, however, the food was late, cold, and bad. "There was much to look at, little to eat, and no women," reports Brant.[51] At one point, the clergy jumped up from table and ran to sing vespers, and when they all sat down again, the new dishes were more vile than the old ones. "If ever one intended to present something really vile or horrible to eat," writes Brant, "it could scarcely have been done with more skill." Some magistrates simply walked out, hoping to find something edible elsewhere, and William cut such a poor figure that only two local nobles turned out, several days later, to joust in his honor. Later, when the bishop complained of the magistrates' massive military precautions for his entry, they replied in icy words: "it pertains to the Senate of the city of Strasbourg to order, mobilize, command, and forbid in their city, just as they please. Enough said."[52]

Through Brant's eyes we see how Bishop William's entry canceled the image created by his pastoral innovations and presented him to the Strasbourgeois as a great Alsatian lord surrounded by warriors. "Thus are Christ's sheep treated throughout the world," writes Brant, "for the proper shepherds have become lords and give their sheep over to the care of hirelings. The sheep are accustomed to fleeing when they see the wolf, so that the

[50]Aulinger, *Bild des Reichstages*, 264-87.

[51]Brant, "Bischof Wilhelm," 291: "es weren vil schauweszen, aber wenig dauweszen, noch minder frouwenweszen," an untranslatable joke. For the next quotation, ibid., 292.

[52]Ibid., 295.

faith is going down the drain."[53] Brant died in 1521, on the eve of the first year of Reformation agitation at Strasbourg.[54]

(3)

The entry of the Emperor Charles V into Augsburg on June 15, 1530, was a much grander affair.[55] At the zenith of his power, Charles came to Germany fresh from his coronation by the pope at Bologna, and he intended to settle the German question at the Imperial Diet of Augsburg. Clemens Sender (1475-ca. 1536), an Augsburg Benedictine and Fugger client, witnessed this entry and described it in his chronicles.[56]

Charles came to Augsburg as his grandfather Maximilian had so often come: from the Tyrol down the Lech River to the Swabian metropolis. With him came an enormous horde, the variety and splendor of which displayed him as a true world ruler: courtiers and clergy – Spaniards, Italians, Netherlanders, and Germans – and more than two hundred princes, counts, and barons "from many lands," a thousand mercenary infantry to police Augsburg during the Diet, a bodyguard of three hundred men, and two hundred Spanish hunting dogs.[57] At his side rode King Ferdinand, his brother, in whose entourage rode nobles from all the Austrian lands from Silesia and Hungary to Alsace, followed by two cardinals, two Counts Palatine, two dukes of Bavaria with five hundred riders in full armor, several bishops, a papal legate, and the foreign ambassadors.

As at Strasbourg in 1507, armed burghers went out to meet the guests – 1,000 armed guildsmen and 200 horse, led by their mayors – but they did not go alone.[58] Electors John of Saxony and Joachim of Brandenburg rode out with 200 and 150 horse respectively, while behind them came Landgrave Philip of Hesse in the midst of 120 crossbowmen dressed in gray. On the Hessians' arms could be seen the motto V.D.M.I.E, which the Protestants eagerly explained to mean "God's Word endures forever (*Verbum dei manet in eternum*)," though the Catholics joked that it really meant "And you must get out of town (*vnd du mußt ins elend*)." When the two processions met, the

---

[53]Ibid., 296.

[54]Jean Rott and Marc Lienhard, "Die Anfänge der evangelischen Predigt in Strassburg und ihr erstes Manifest: Der Aufruf des Karmeliterlesemeisters Tilman von Lyn (Anfang 1522)," in Marijn de Kroon and Friedhelm Krüger, eds., *Bucer und seine Zeit: Forschungsbeiträge und Bibliographie* (Wiesbaden: Franz Steiner Verlag, 1976), 54-73.

[55]See Aulinger, *Bild des Reichstages*, 329-39.

[56]Clemens Sender, "Die Chronik von Clemens Sender von den ältesten Zeiten der Stadt bis zum Jahre 1536," in *Chroniken der deutschen Städte*, vol. 23 (Leipzig: Salomon Hirzel, 1894; reprinted, Göttingen: Vandenhoeck & Ruprecht, 1966), 252-79. On Sender, see Carla Karmer-Schlette, *Vier Augsburger Chronisten der Reformationszeit: Die Behandlung und Deutung der Zeitgeschichte bei Clemens Sender, Wilhelm Rem, Georg Preu und Paul Hektor Mair,* Historische Studien, no. 421 (Lübeck: Matthiesen Verlag, 1970).

[57]Sender, *Chronik*, 264-67.

[58]Ibid., 268-74.

town clerk welcomed the emperor, and all the guns and cannon were fired in greeting. Then the united party paraded into the city, Charles's mercenaries in the van and the emperor, flanked by his brother and the cardinal-legate, riding under the red-white-green canopy of the city, carried by six magistrates. Straight into the city's heart they rode, to the Perlach tower by the town hall, where the bishop and clergy took Charles in charge and led him to the cathedral. The party was thousands upon thousands strong, horses and armed men, so many that the guild militias could never have contained them. After the Te Deum in the cathedral, to which "none of the common folk was admitted,"[59] Charles went to the episcopal palace on foot, accompanied by his brother, the king, the cardinal-legate, "and all the princes and lords."[60] There he resided for about four months, while his presence both enriched the burghers and reminded them of their dependence on him and the world he represented.

This tremendous entry displayed to all present – burghers, princes, lords, bishops, priests, soliders, and servants – the wealth, splendor, and might of the Habsburg world-empire and the House of Austria; it also revealed the opposition between Charles and the Catholic princes and bishops, on one side, and the Evangelical princes, on the other. The magistrates had to open their city's heart to the rulers of the entire Holy Roman Empire, both friend and foe, and allow it to become the stage on which the first major test between the religious parties took place. After the Diet of Augsburg, the German Reformation drama unfolded scene-by-scene through the armed negotiations of the 1530s, the Schmalkaldic War in 1546-47, and the princes' revolt in 1552 to its end in the Religious Peace of Augsburg in 1555. Not even the most astute Augsburger could have seen in 1530, however, that the Habsburg world-empire would win each struggle but the last one.

(4)

How do the two entries compare as political theater? They certainly tell different stories. The Strasbourgeois confronted their bishop as a rival, whose rights on the burghers' ground were strictly limited to those of a guest, and whose military entourage they carefully barred from the city's political heart. Bishop William's entry thus unfolded as a drama of regional politics, slightly tinged by William's residual claims as Strasbourg's chief pastor. The story contained, however, no ambiguities: the commune believed itself to be at least the bishop's equal, and in their own city, he was merely their guest.

The Augsburg entry of Charles V tells a story of a city open to the great world – German, Italian, Netherlandish, and Spanish – on the wealth, power, and favor of which the city's prosperity depended. The powers of the outside world rode straight into Augsburg's heart, and the city became, for a while,

---

[59]Ibid., 276, ll. 20-21.
[60]Ibid., 278, ll. 8-9. See Aulinger, *Bild des Reichstages*, 335.

the capital of the Holy Roman Empire and the Habsburg system, and only secondarily the home and citadel of Augsburg's commune.

The ritual entries also tell stories in what they conceal or only partially reveal. The Strasbourg entry reveals the bishop's regional power but conceals that of the House of Austria. It reveals the commune's encroachment on the bishop's ecclesiastical power, but it conceals the inability of civic culture to achieve true religious self-sufficiency. In the throes of the Reformation movement, therefore, Protestantism would fail to conquer the entire Upper Rhenish region, and Strasbourg would be swept by the power of competing religious parties – Zwinglian, Lutheran, and Anabaptist. The entry's story thus contains no hint of the vulnerabilities which would drive Strasbourg into the arms of most unlikely suitors, the Central German princes.[61] Not even the most astute Strasbourgeois could have seen in 1507 that his city would stake its future on such distant cards.

Charles V's entry into Augsburg also revealed and concealed stories. It displayed both the grandeur and the vulnerability of Imperial power: grand in its array of lands reaching from Bohemia to Castile and from Holland to Naples; weak in its ruler's inability to cajole or to coerce the Central German princes from their opposition. As for the clergy, the entry witnessed their parade out from the cathedral to meet Charles; it also showed the papal legate riding in the shadow of Habsburg power. Augsburg's burghers could read from the entry both how the city had prospered through its far-flung trade and the Habsburg connection, and how the church depended on the Imperial protection.

The entry rites, therefore, tell stories both through revelation and through concealment, and the historian of civic culture should study such events as complements and correctives, not as alternatives, to other sources. If read carefully, they do suggest important possibilities. The two entries I have described contain significant clues to the two cities' fates in the Reformation era. The Alsatian metropolis pulled away from its regional rootedness to enter the Schmalkaldic League in 1531; the Swabian city turned from its Habsburg connection toward the same course a few years later. That road led to defeat and humiliation, but also to very different consequences for the two cities. Strasbourg, with its regionally based economy, its relatively united burghers, and its distance from the major principalities, survived the defeat with its government intact and its Protestant church only briefly disrupted by a Catholic restoration.[62] Augsburg, with its extremely vulnerable

[61]See my forthcoming study, "Godly Republics: The Domestication of Religion in the German Urban Reformation," in R. Po-chia Hsia, ed., *The People and the German Reformation: Approaches in the Social History of Religion* (Ithaca: Cornell University Press, 1988), 14-32.

[62]On Strasbourg's fate, see Weyrauch, *Konfessionelle Krise und soziale Stabilität*; on Augsburg's fate, see Eberhard Naujoks, ed., *Kaiser Karl V. und die Zunftverfassung: Ausgewählte Aktenstücke zu den Verfassungsänderungen in den oberdeutschen Reichsstädten (1547-1556)*, Veröffentlichungen der Kommission für geschichtliche Landeskunde in Baden-Württemberg, series A, no. 36 (Stuttgart: Kohlhammer Verlag, 1984).

export trade, its deep social divisions, its proximity to the Bavarian and Austrian lands, and its financial ties to the Habsburgs, lost its guild constitution and endured a permanent Catholic restoration. Some clues to these fates can be read from the two entries, which portray two quite different degrees of dependence on the extra-communal world.[63] They thus suggest the utility of political rituals for the study of civic culture.

(5)

Why has an approach so simple and so helpful made so little headway in writing on the German-speaking cities? The simplest answer is that German historical circles have not shared in the appropriation of anthropology's insights and methods.[64] True, but why is this so? There is the obvious answer that anthropology's reputation was destroyed in the Nazi era, but I have two further suggestions. The first is that history in Germany has been a predominantly Protestant discipline. This is indicated not only by its preoccupation with textual study and hermeneutical questions – the supremacy of words – but also by its emphasis on history as the story of consciousness.[65] The essentially Protestant character of this sensibility is suggested by the observation that the Reformation replaced the Catholic norm of *lex orandi, lex credendi,* with the Protestant *lex docendi, lex orandi.*[66] Wolfgang Weber's work on the social recruitment of professors of history in the German-speaking world between 1810 and 1970 gives sociological underpinning to the view that in Germany history has been a fundamentally Protestant discipline.[67] From these roots, perhaps, arises a disinclination to regard European Christianity, especially post-Reformation Christianity, in anthropological rather than theological or institutional terms. My second suggestion concerns the purely European context of German historiography. Historical studies in France, England, most of Asia and Africa, and North and South America stand very much under the sign of the collapse of European imperial rule over non-Europeans; but the German-speaking peoples did not experience this kind of imperial triumph and misery to any significant degree. There is little writing on world history in Germany today,

---

[63]This confirms the suggestions – made fifty years ago – of Hans Baron, "Religion and Politics in the German Imperial Cities during the Reformation," *The English Historical Review* 52 (1937): 405-27, 614-33.

[64]There are signs that this is changing, so much so that Hermann Bausinger recently warned the historians against an uncritical grasp at folklore. Hermann Bausinger, "Traditionale Welten: Kontinuität und Wandel in der Volkskultur," *Historische Zeitschrift* 241 (1985): 265-87.

[65]See Georg G. Iggers, *The German Conception of History: The National Tradition of Historical Thought from Herder to the Present,* rev. ed. (Middletown, Conn.: Wesleyan University Press, 1983), 3-28.

[66]See Brady, "Godly Republics," 21.

[67]Wolfgang Weber, *Priester der Klio: Historisch-sozialwissenschaftliche Studien zur Herkunft und Karriere deutscher Historiker und zur Geschichte der Geschichtswissenschaft 1810-1970,* Europäische Hochschulschriften, ser. 3, no. 216 (Frankfurt: Peter Lang, 1984).

and the grand theorists of the past two decades – Wallerstein, Wolf, Philip Jones, McNeill, and Crosby – have had little impact on historical studies there.[68] These two factors, the Protestant origins and character of the historical discipline and the intramural European context of German history, tend to preserve the gulf between pre- and post-Reformation history and between ritual religion and doctrinal religion. They may help to explain why historians of German cities in the age of Renaissance and Reformation have been slow to turn to ritual as an entryway to civic culture or to acknowledge that, sometimes, actions do speak louder than words.

---

[68]Wolfgang Reinhard, *Geschichite der europäischen Expansion,* 3 vols. (Stuttgart: Kohlhammer, 1983-88), with more volumes to come, impresses by its singularity; it is the only major German work in the recent general literature on European empires and colonialism.

Allegory of Good Government with Nuremberg in the Background

The Virgin on the Street Corner:
The Place of the Sacred in
Italian Cities

Edward Muir

ON NEARLY EVERY STREET CORNER in the back alleys of Venice, one can still find the Virgin Mary.[1] She usually presents herself as a modest statue or crude painting, or sometimes only a faded picture postcard set up within a niche or frame (*capitello*) on the outside wall of a house or church. Thousands of images of Mary, the saints, and Christ proliferated throughout the city, encouraged by religious orders and parish priests but most often produced by neighborhood or private devotions. Beginning in 1450 the republic charged a local patrician with responsibility for watching over these images, and in the residential neighborhoods they still flourish. Historians can never recapture all their functions and meanings in the little and great dramas of urban activity, but these Madonnas and saints had many lives. Some depicted the patron of the parish church, extending the sacrality of the church outward through a neighborhood cult; others worked miracles, cured the afflicted, and guarded against plague; some succored the poor, protected against street crime, or discouraged blasphemy; and most reminded the living of their obligations to pray for the dead.[2] Saintly images created a setting where reverential behavior was appropriate, and the ubiquity of images may point to a social style characterized by formality and the pervasiveness of ritual and theatricality in daily life. Intercessors with the divine permeated urban spaces in many Italian cities to such a degree that rigid distinctions between sacred

---

[1]Portions of this article have been adapted from an article co-authored with Ronald F. E. Weissman, "Social and Symbolic Places in Renaissance Venice and Florence," in *The Power of Place,* ed. John Agnew and James Duncan (London and Boston: Allen & Unwin, 1989). I am grateful to Professor Weissman for his many insights which have contributed to this article and also wish to thank Patricia Fortini Brown, Linda L. Carroll, Natalie Zemon Davis, and Lionel Rothkrug for their criticisms and suggestions. Prof. Rothkrug emphasizes the significance of the difference between the adjectives *holy* and *sacred,* a distinction which the Germans lacked. See his "German Holiness and Western Sanctity in Medieval and Modern History," *Historical Reflections* 15 (1988): 169, an article Prof. Rothkrug kindly sent me before its publication. In Italian the distinction would be between *santo* and *sacro,* but Italian usage does not always correspond exactly to the English differences between holy and sacred, and in both languages the terms are commonly used interchangeably. Since this article is about the social and spatial context of religious images, relics, and objects, exact semantic distinctions create the appearance of a greater theological precision than is possible given the character of the evidence. I will follow, therefore, contemporary Catholic usage of the terms *holy* and *sacred* and do not intend to imply a precise distinction between them.

[2]Antonio Niero, "Per la storia della pietà popolare veneziana: Capitelli e immagini di santi a Venezia," *Ateneo Veneto,* n.s., 8 (1970): 262-67 and idem, "Il culto dei santi nell'arte popolare," in A. Niero, G. Musolino, and S. Tramontin, *Sanctità a Venezia* (Venice: Edizioni dello Studium Cattolico Veneziano, 1972), 229-89. Cf. M. Nani Mocenigo, "I capitelli veneziani," *Le Tre Venezie* 17 (1942): 224-27 and Paolo Toschi, "Mostra di arte religiosa popolare," *Lares* 13 (1942): 195-97.

and profane, so typical of the Reformation, must have seemed alien, even irreligious, to many who lived in towns magically tied together by little shrines. Italian towns, moreover, were themselves mystical bodies, a corporation both in the legal sense and the literal one of a number of persons united in one body, nourished and protected by a civic patron saint.[3] Citizenship was not just a legal distinction but one of the principal social influences in identity formation.

But situating little holy places about the city like fountains hardly guaranteed appropriate behavior. In an attempt to reduce street violence, Udine followed such a strategy by erecting images at the entrances of each quarter and on certain houses and by encouraging neighborhood cults, but the city fathers largely failed to pacify their community.[4] Local context determined the social significance of holy places, and the multiple touchstones of the sacred in Italian cities – street-corner Madonnas, parish churches, monasteries, confraternity chapels, even government buildings – created tangled, overlapping, and conflicted religious commitments among believers which resembled the agonistic character of their social lives.[5] In the relationship between place and the sacred, one finds contradictory tendencies – some that promoted tensions and urban conflicts, others that fostered spiritual community. By focusing on the relationship between social behavior and the character of the holy, one can see both how humans create sacred objects and places and how these influence behavior.

In her essay, "The Sacred and the Body Social in Sixteenth-Century Lyon," Natalie Zemon Davis analyzes the symbolic configurations of urban religion and treats Protestantism and Catholicism as "two languages which, among many uses, could describe, mark and interpret urban life, and in particular urban space, urban time and the urban community."[6] Whether or not the sacred could be localized in space became, after all, a major issue in the theological conflict between Catholics and Protestants, the former insisting on the divine presence in the Eucharist and treating relics as special objects of devotion, the latter refusing to acknowledge such an impious mixing of spirit and matter. But the dispute was never purely theological. Relations with the sacred provide an idealized pattern of earthly social

---

[3]Hans Conrad Peyer, *Stadt und Stadtpatron im Mittelalterlichen Italien* (Zurich: Europa Verlag, 1955). Ernst H. Kantorowicz, *The King's Two Bodies: A Study in Medieval Political Theology* (Princeton: Princeton University Press, 1957).

[4]Antonio Battistella, "Udine nel secolo XVI: La religione e i provvedimenti economico-sociale," *Memorie storiche forogiuliesi* 20 (1924): 5.

[5]Ronald F. E. Weissman, "Reconstructing Renaissance Sociology: The 'Chicago School' and the Study of Renaissance Society," in *Persons in Groups: Social Behavior as Identity Formation in Medieval and Renaissance Europe,* ed. Richard C. Trexler (Binghamton, N.Y.: Center for Medieval and Early Renaissance Studies, 1985), 44-45.

[6]Natalie Zemon Davis, "The Sacred and the Body Social in Sixteenth-Century Lyon," *Past and Present* 90 (1981): 42.

relations, and changes in attitudes toward the sacred altered the means by which Renaissance townspeople might form their social identity.[7] Even before the Reformation many Italian cities exhibited religious heteroglossia, to adopt Bakhtin's term, multiple languages through which various social groups approached and understood the location of the sacred.[8] Structured in part by dogma and in part by the relations between clergy and laity, a language of religious symbolism is also the product of the "distinctive experience of the people who use it."[9] It is this peculiarly lay language of the sacred that wants recapturing, an argot discovered in what Angelo Torre calls the "consumption of devotions."[10] Despite many dialectal variants, two forms, I would suggest, dominated in Italian cities.

One might be called the prophetic language, unstable in time and space, appearing, disappearing, and reappearing according to the vicissitudes of events. Prophecies played a major role in lay culture, as Ottavia Niccoli has shown in her analysis of the pamphlets sold by itinerant ballad singers and preachers after piazza performances. During the political disintegration of Italy after 1494, editions of prophecies multiplied, but after the Peace of Bologna in 1530, they virtually disappeared, except perhaps in Venice.[11] The notorious plasticity of prophecies, subject to highly imaginative reinterpretations, made them alluring in unstable times but apt to evanesce after a short time.

The second kind of sacred language, and for our purposes the more important, might be called the iconic, in which holiness tended to adhere to an object or a place, sometimes in direct defiance of theological doctrine. The sacred presented itself in temporal cycles rather than with apocalyptic finality and had a more fixed relationship to space than the prophetic language, although all venerated objects were potentially mobile and some actually so, regularly moving about the city in processions. The iconic

[7]William A. Christian, Jr., *Apparitions in Late Medieval and Renaissance Spain* (Princeton: Princeton University Press, 1981).

[8]Mikhail Bakhtin, *Rabelais and His World* (Cambridge, Mass.: MIT Press, 1968). Katarina Clark and Michael Holquist, *Mikhail Bakhtin* (Cambridge, Mass.: Harvard University Press, 1984). Tzvetan Todorov, *Mikhail Bakhtin: The Dialogical Principle* (Minneapolis: University of Minnesota Press, 1984), 56, 72-73, 77.

[9]Davis, "The Sacred and the Body Social," 67.

[10]"Il consumo di devozioni: rituali e potere nelle campagne Piemontesi nella prima metà del Settecento," *Quaderni storici*, n.s., 58 (1985): 181-82.

[11]Ottavia Niccoli, "Profezie in piazza: Note sul profetismo popolare nell'Italia del primo Cinquecento," *Quaderni storici* 41 (1979): 514-15. Cf. idem, "Il re dei morti sul campo di Agnadello," *Quaderni storici* 51 (1982): 929-58. I have not yet been able to consult Niccoli's new book on prophecies. On the survival of a prophetic tradition in Venice after the period Niccoli discusses, see Marion Leathers Kuntz, *Guglielmo Postello e la "Vergine Veneziana": Appunti storici sulla vita spirituale dell'Ospedaletto nel Cinquecento* (Venice: Centro Tedesco di Studi Veneziani, Quaderni no. 21, 1981). John Martin discussed a late sixteenth-century millennialist group of Venetian artisans in "The Sect of Benedetto Corazzaro," a paper presented at the Sixteenth Century Studies Conference, Tempe, Arizona, October 30, 1987.

language offered citizens immediate and personal intimacy with the saints rather than the future collective salvation promised by the prophets, and images and relics had intensely meaningful relationships with urban spaces, not only because the devout wished to see and touch such objects, but also because the moving of images and relics through city streets in processions celebrated *communitas*. The perpetuation of the procession's salubrious effects was one of the objectives in erecting images of the Virgin in public places. Virgins in many locations created a different kind of procession, one actively experienced by citizens as they walked about following their daily affairs.[12]

The meanings conveyed and behaviors evoked by these images, however, could hardly be controlled or predicted. In particular, women may have reacted very differently from men to the Virgin, and since Jews could not be expected to respond as Christians, authorities had to face the reality that their cities were never fully united. In Venice and other cities where ghettos were established, residential segregation created zones free from Catholic notions of sacred spaces, and the movement of non-Christian residents about the rest of the city was carefully restricted, since they would not be influenced toward righteousness by the Virgin Mary or Saint Francis. In a few cases Jews were even allowed to destroy Christian images painted on the walls of their houses, although the reaction of the Christian populace to such perceived defilements might be quite violent.[13] Despite the variety of behavior stimulated by such images, established norms defined appropriate responses.

Most Italian urban laymen and women were likely to seek communion with the saints through a proper self-presentation rather than through an agonized Augustinian self-examination on the issue of sincerity. In his recent historical anthropology of Italy, the "land of façades," Peter Burke proposes what he calls the "sincerity threshold." Higher in the North of Europe than in the South, the sincerity threshold operates on a "kind of sliding scale . . . so that a stress on sincerity in a given culture tends to be associated with a lack of emphasis on other qualities, such as courtesy. . . . Paradoxical as it may seem on the surface, sincerity cultures need a greater measure of self-deception than the rest – since we are all actors – while 'theatre cultures', as we may call them, are able to cultivate the self-awareness they value less."[14] Burke seems to mean that it is more important in the North than the South to make statements on intention correspond to overt actions. In

---

[12]Niero counted 406 images of the Virgin in the streets of Venice. "Il culto dei santi," 264-85.

[13]Michele Luzzatti, "Ebrei, chiesa locale, 'Principe' e popolo: Due episodi di distruzione di immagini sacre alla fine del Quattrocento," *Quaderni storici* 54 (1983): 847-77.

[14]Peter Burke, *The Historical Anthropology of Early Modern Italy: Essays on Perception and Communication* (Cambridge: Cambridge University Press, 1987), 12-13. Cf. David I. Kertzer, *Ritual, Politics, and Power* (New Haven: Yale University Press, 1988).

the southern theater cultures, norms are more often established in behavioral rather than verbal terms; thus, the issue of intention and sincerity is less likely to arise. The goal of social relations in a theater culture is similar to that of dramatic acting: to create the appearance of effortless, natural behavior even though all may be calculated. Such an emphasis on appearances correlates with the belief, which anthropologists find characteristic of Mediterranean societies, that "seeing" is the only reliable source of knowledge.[15] The Virgin hovering in every street required a performance, and even for the pious the most important thing was to bring it off.

Thus, when approaching the various sacred images and objects, the devout conveyed reverence through a demonstration that one had been properly socialized.[16] To calm a riotous crowd, priests would proceed through the city with a miracle-working image or relic. But there also remained a deep ambiguity about the range of behaviors acceptable in the presence of the sacred. Its separation from the corruption of business activity (seemingly required of Christians by the example of Christ's casting out the money-changers from the Temple) was often transgressed in Renaissance Italy, where the market needed holy objects to facilitate business and where, for many, religious behavior was merely another form of negotiation. Requiring an atmosphere of trust for the extension of credit and the firming of business deals, traders and artisans sought to sanctify their commercial dealings by notarizing, signing, and witnessing their contracts in a church where the parties might be invested with a fear of divine punishment for breaking their word.[17] One of the oldest standing churches in Venice, for example, is in the center of the Rialto market, and elsewhere saints' shrines became the site for market fairs. Such profane uses provoked protests from reforming preachers, such as Bernardino of Siena, but they enjoyed little success in isolating churches from the mundane, at least until the Counter-Reformation.

Ambiguity about the proper use of churches, of course, reached back to the concept of sacred space peculiar to Christianity. Peter Brown has argued that one of the distinguishing characteristics of early Christianity was its belief in the mobility of the sacred.[18] Christians replaced sacred wells, caves, and trees with Christ's eucharistic body and the corpses of martyrs for the

[15]David D. Gilmore, "Anthropology of the Mediterranean Area," *Annual Reviews in Anthropology* 11 (1982): 197-98.

[16]Richard C. Trexler, *Public Life in Renaissance Florence* (New York: Academic Press, 1980), 45-128. Cf. Moshe Barasch, *Gestures of Despair in Medieval and Early Renaissance Art* (New York: New York University Press, 1976). Michael Baxandall, *Painting and Experience in Fifteenth-Century Italy: A Primer in the Social History of Pictorial Style* (Oxford: Clarendon Press, 1976), 56-71.

[17]Trexler, *Public Life,* 111-12, 263-70.

[18]Peter Brown, *The Cult of the Saints: Its Rise and Function in Latin Christianity* (Chicago: University of Chicago Press, 1981), 86-105.

faith, objects which could be moved from place to place. Churches and monasteries were holy because of the ceremony of consecration but also because of the activities they permitted and the objects they contained: "The place does not sanctify the man but the man the place," and the church is not essential to the relic but the relic to the church. In devotional practice holiness was revealed in gradations of intensity: some things were more holy than others. Even Saint Bernardino argued that a sacrilege against a holy object was far worse than one simply perpetrated within a holy place.[19]

Such distinctions manifested themselves in numerous ways. *Ex votos* clustered around a reliquary or a miracle-working image reflected a sensitivity to the location and intensity of the holy, and pilgrimages encouraged belief in the efficacy of gaining access to sacred objects.[20] Lay devouts often seem to have considered images as signs that indicated the presence of the saint rather than as symbols that brought the saint's spiritual qualities to mind. The impulse to decorate and embellish churches (especially altars) may have come in part from an underlying anxiety about the mobility of the sacred. A saint who was ill-treated or forced to dwell in shabby surroundings might just allow his or her body to be "translated" elsewhere. And the theft of relics was always a danger. Many of Venice's most important relics, including the body of Saint Mark and the head of Saint George, had in fact been stolen in North Africa or the Near East and brought to Venice by traveling merchants and crusaders.[21] Anxious about such possibilities, Italian citizens and clerics sought to fix sacred objects in particular places by arguing – often through hagiography, pious legends, and apparitions – that a saint favored a certain place or church. The emanations of ecclesiastical buildings confused spirit and matter in a manner that would become especially offensive to reformers. Although Catholic theology placed strict limits on sanctified objects and rejected as pagan the notion that places could be sacred by themselves, popular practice tended nonetheless to create sacred places. Leon Battista Alberti, who saw all spaces in the mathematics of proportionality and geometry, was puzzled by the mystic hierarchy of places created, he thought, by popular beliefs. But in recognizing how widespread such attitudes were, he conceded that the architect must prescribe fixed places for religious statues.

I wonder how most people can so credit the opinions transmitted by our ancestors that it is believed that a certain picture of a god [or saint] situated in one place hears prayers while a statue of the same god a short distance away is unwilling to heed appeals? Not only

[19]Quotation from Francesco da Barberino as translated in Trexler, *Public Life*, 52-54.

[20]Cf. Burke, *Historical Anthropology*, 209-10.

[21]Edward Muir, *Civic Ritual in Renaissance Venice* (Princeton: Princeton University Press, 1981), 78-102. Patrick J. Geary, *Furta Sacra: Thefts of Relics in the Central Middle Ages* (Princeton: Princeton University Press, 1978).

that but when these same, most venerated images are moved to a different place, the people lose faith in them and quit praying to them. Such statues, therefore, must have permanent, dignified locations set aside for them alone.[22]

Complex social patterns and traditions enmeshed sacred places in a profusion of ambiguities that forced concessions to popular beliefs, which were themselves often highly creative. At the present state of research perhaps all that can be achieved is a very tentative suggestion of the varieties of these relationships. To do so, one might compare Venice, Florence, Naples, and Udine. As often happens in Italian history, systematic comparisons are difficult, especially because research in these cities has concentrated on different periods. Given the diversity of Italian regions, moreover, it would be absurd to argue that these cities are representative or typical, but they do encompass a calculated variety by including two major city-republics and two cities linked by formal feudal ties to the countryside and dominated by a "foreign" power. By the end of the sixteenth century Naples was the largest of these cities, indeed the largest of Christendom. With a population of 280,000, it was twice the size of Venice, three times that of Rome, four times that of Florence, and nearly twenty times the population of Udine.[23] Within each of these cities diverse social groups expressed their devotion in various ways. Diversity seems to have been most dramatic in Naples, least evident in Venice. Particularly before 1530, Florence displayed a range of competing forms, and the laity of Udine lacked a deeply-rooted Christian language of the sacred, at least in comparison to that of other Italian towns.

As a "theater state" Venice, like Counter-Reformation Rome, most effectively interpreted an iconic language for the purposes of maintaining public order.[24] The doges succeeded in permanently capturing Saint Mark for themselves, and although Mark was the patron of all Venetians, after the fourteenth century he was so surrounded by institutional barriers that he was limited to silent service at the placid center of the state cult. In Venice processional routes included the whole city and tied the neighborhoods to a ceremonial center where a vast architectural frame set apart ritual performances. In Piazza San Marco, as in Rome's Piazza San Pietro, a large public square retained a special character derived from the sacred activities

---

[22]Leon Battista Alberti, *L'Architettura [De Re Aedificatoria]*, ed. Giovanni Orlandi (Milan: Edizioni il Polifilo, 1966), 2: 661-63 (book 7, chap. 17). The translation is mine. The passage is analyzed in Joan Gadol, *Leon Battista Alberti: Universal Man of the Early Renaissance* (Chicago: University of Chicago Press, 1969), 150-51. Also see Lionel Rothkrug, "Holy Shrines, Religious Dissonance and Satan in the Origins of the German Reformation," *Historical Reflections* 14 (1987): 146 and idem, "German Holiness," 161-64.

[23]Fernand Braudel, *The Mediterranean and the Mediterranean World in the Age of Philip II*, 2 vols. (New York: Harper & Row, 1972), 1: 345.

[24]Cf. Clifford Geertz, *Negara: The Theatre State in Nineteenth-Century Bali* (Princeton: Princeton University Press, 1980), and Burke, *Historical Anthropology*, 10, 174.

that took place there, and through an escalation of magnificences during the late sixteenth century, these two cities defiantly reasserted the incorporation of the sacred into worldly spaces.[25]

The salient feature of Venice's distinctive cityscape was its center, where the most prestigious and powerful institutions clustered around the Doge's Palace and adjacent Basilica of Saint Mark. Exhibiting weaker forms of neighborhood organization than in other cities and a high level of residential mobility evident as early as the thirteenth century, Venetian parishes played a small role in forming citizens' social identity.[26] Males from patrician families pursued rewards and influence by competing for civic offices and seeking government favors; thus in Venice patronage was more city-wide and less neighborhood-bound than in Florence, Genoa, or probably most other Italian cities.

Venetian patronage, however, may have been peculiarly sex- and class-specific. Dennis Romano has suggested that Venetian patrician women, in contrast to their husbands, developed well-articulated local patronage networks largely because women were secluded in their palaces and seldom appeared in public beyond the parish confines. Romano has found evidence that lower-class women in the fourteenth century frequently chose a patrician woman from their own parish to act as executor of their wills whereas lower-class men almost never designated a male patrician to serve in this delicate capacity. Neighborhood patronage among males in Venice fell to the better-off commoners, especially to the secondary legal elite of *cittadini*, who dominated, for example, the parish-level priesthood. A Venetian priest's influence came less perhaps from his role as confessor, spiritual advisor, and preacher than from his involvement in the secular world. Parish priests served as executors of wills, held the power of attorney, acted as notaries, invested in commercial ventures, and were particularly valued as sources for small loans.[27] Appparently indifferent to parish affairs, the upper class male Venetian experienced the sacred by joining a city-wide confraternity or by acting as a lay patron for a monastery or mendicant church as did Italians of other cities. In fact, a significant minority of wealthy Venetians sought burial

[25]Muir, *Civic Ritual*. Charles Stinger, *The Renaissance in Rome* (Bloomington: Indiana University Press, 1985). Burke, *Historical Anthropology*, 168-82.

[26]Stanley Chojnacki, "In Search of the Venetian Patriciate: Families and Factions in the Fourteenth Century," in *Renaissance Venice*, ed. J. R. Hale (London: Faber and Faber, 1973), 59-60. Rona Goffen, *Piety and Patronage in Renaissance Venice: Bellini, Titian, and the Franciscans* (New Haven: Yale University Press, 1986), 27-28.

[27]Dennis Romano, *Patricians and Popolani: The Social Foundations of the Venetian Renaissance State* (Baltimore: Johns Hopkins University Press, 1987), 91-102, 131-40. Romano has further discussed the decline of Venetian parishes after 1297 in a superb paper, "Politics and Parishes in Early Renaissance Venice," presented at the annual conference of the Renaissance Society of America, New York, March 18, 1988. Also see Richard Mackenney, *Tradesmen and Traders: The World of the Guilds in Venice and Europe, c. 1250-c. 1650* (Totowa, N.J.: Barnes & Noble Books, 1987), 47.

sites outside of their parish and paid for tombs in convents, monasteries, or mendicant churches often located at some distance from the family house or palace.[28]

For the various annual feasts the Venetian doge and signoria attended special masses throughout the city, and in comparison to other cities, especially Florence, Venice more often commemorated historical events important for the entire city in its civic liturgy and less often recognized local patrons or important ecclesiastics.[29] Lay officials exemplified their control by dominating sacred places. Unlike Florence, neither parishes, *sestieri* (quarters), nor any other neighborhood division was ever represented after the fourteenth century in a Venetian ritual. The constituent elements of the Corpus Christi rite in Venice, for example, were corporate groups, especially the confraternities, which were carefully regulated by the Council of Ten, and the greatest annual festival, the marriage of the doge to the sea, engaged secular and ecclesiastical hierarchies, arranged according to a rigid protocol of precedence, in a mystical union with the watery environment.[30] In comparison to other Italian cities except perhaps Rome, Venice displayed the most precise hierarchy of sacred and profane spaces, a time-bound, sometimes inverted, occasionally subverted hierarchy, but nevertheless a symbolic scheme which organized much of the urban plan. In most other cities the relative strength of private power ensured that private groups would successfully compete with public authority by elevating their private spaces to a high symbolic position.

The goal of the public control of space, to be perhaps too crudely simple, was to influence the loyalties and obligations of individuals. To accomplish this, the sacred was employed iconically to work a miraculous restructuring of social obligations in a way impossible merely through the legal expansion of public domination over urban spaces. In Venice, the necessity of controlling a difficult habitat, that ever recalcitrant space that would disappear into the sea without consistent intervention, led to the subordination of neighborhood-based loyalties in the interest of collective ecologic survival. Only the highly personalized street Virgins and saints had strong neighborhood ties, but the central government encouraged devotion to these images and they never seem to have threatened the hegemony of Saint Mark, who had a greater, more unifying, and more lasting hold on Venetian loyalties than anyone or anything else. The civic triumphed in Venice, not completely, perhaps, but completely enough to allow centrally located institutions to dominate the Venetian social and spatial order.

[28]Romano, *Patricians and Popolani,* 102-18; Mackenney, *Tradesmen and Traders,* 56-61; Brian Pullan, *Rich and Poor in Renaissance Venice: The Social Institutions of a Catholic State, to 1620* (Oxford: Basil Blackwell, 1971), 33-196.

[29]Muir, *Civic Ritual,* 212-23.

[30]Ibid., 119-34.

Multicentered Florence, in contrast, had various sources of social power and a physical geography with several distinct and dominant visual foci.[31] Major institutions were dispersed throughout the city, creating a physical geography that was visually and conceptually chaotic. Up to the end of the fifteenth century Florence was the home of prophetic publications in Italy, a sign of instability furthered by the absence of a single source of the sacred that triumphed over all others.[32] In Florence neighborhood clients were still the base for a political career, and in contrast to Venice there was a greater tendency for patricians to identify with their neighborhood by sponsoring works for the local church, as the Medici did so famously with San Lorenzo.[33]

Outside of the political class, Florentines found their most vital daily contacts in their face-to-face relationships in the neighborhood piazza. These neighborhoods, like those in Venice, did not conform to the stereotype of the medieval city in which members of the same craft lived close together in the same district. Most neighborhoods were socially heterogeneous, containing both the palaces of the rich and the tenements of the poor, and members of many different trades. With a few exceptions, industry was organized on such a small scale that artisans in the same trade had no special incentive to live in close proximity to one another. Apart from ethnic ghettos of foreign workers, residential segregation was normal only for the artisans in a few specialized crafts, so that the majority lived among and married the daughters of craftsmen in other professions, although during the fifteenth century, as Samuel Cohn has argued, members of the Florentine working class may have begun to experience higher rates of parish, if not occupational, endogamy than before.[34] The extended family, although it had lost its thirteenth-century corporate status, remained a vital social unit, serving as the organizing force behind Florentine commerce, qualifying one for membership in guilds and other corporate groups, continuing as a component

[31]My analysis of Florence closely follows Muir and Weissman, "Social and Symbolic Places," and is particularly indebted to Ronald F. E. Weissman, *Ritual Brotherhood in Renaissance Florence* (New York: Academic Press, 1982), and Trexler, *Public Life.* Also see Giorgio Simoncini, *Città e società nel Rinascimento,* 2 vols. (Turin: Einaudi, 1974), and Richard Goldthwaite, *The Building of Renaissance Florence* (Baltimore: Johns Hopkins University Press, 1980).

[32]Donald Weinstein, *Savonarola and Florence: Prophecy and Patriotism in the Renaissance* (Princeton: Princeton University Press, 1970). Niccoli, "Profezie in piazza," 505.

[33]Dale Kent and F. W. Kent, *Neighbours and Neighbourhood in Renaissance Florence: The District of the Red Lion in the Fifteenth Century* (New York: J. Augustin, 1982). Cf. Goldthwaite, *Building of Renaissance Florence,* 12-13.

[34]Samuel Kline Cohn, *The Laboring Classes in Renaissance Florence* (New York: Academic Press, 1980).

of prestige, and influencing one's honor, status, and ability to participate in urban politics.[35]

Neighborhood could also generate strong animosities and jealousies, for the piazza served as a common stage bringing together a citizen's many, sometimes incompatible, roles of kinsman, friend, political ally, tax assessor, business partner, client, parishioner. Managing them and maintaining numerous potentially conflicting loyalties was an arduous task in which the most valuable social commodity of honor could be won or lost.[36] The specific role of neighborhood in social life varied by class, by status, by age, and almost certainly by sex. For the Florentine citizens who were politically eligible and wealthy enough to pay taxes, the *gonfaloni* and quarters of the town had significant meaning. It was, after all, around the banner of the *gonfalon* that each male citizen assembled under threat of fines during the city's chief civic pageant, the feast day of Saint John the Baptist. For the socially marginal – the poor and the working classes, adolescents, and women – neighborhood boundaries were more fluid and amorphous, and could include piazza, street corner, or alley but generally coalesced around the parish. In the fourteenth century and again in the late fifteenth century the *popolo minuto* organized neighborhood festive bands which staged mock and occasionally real turf battles during feast days. By the middle of the sixteenth century, the parish, newly energized by the forces of Catholic reform, was the only remaining source of corporate solidarity, in the wake of the collapse of *gonfaloni* and guilds.[37]

As a counterweight to neighborhood loyalties, Florentine city fathers promoted civism with the cult of Saint John the Baptist, whose popularity spread from the Romanesque baptistry where all of Florence went to be baptized. The baptistry and the adjacent cathedral became the spiritual center of Florence, and the beginning and end for most processions. In addition, government buildings, especially the city hall, represented political salvation through the display of sacred signs and symbols. A raised platform in front of Florence's hall, for example, became an altar during civic ceremonies, thereby directly imputing divine sanction to public authority.[38]

The mobility of the sacred and the annual liturgical cycle conspired to give every major neighborhood and its chief lay patrons a chance to demonstrate their charisma to the entire city, a chance to link the collective

---

[35]Francis William Kent, *Household and Lineage in Renaissance Florence: The Family Life of the Capponi, Ginori, and Rucellai* (Princeton: Princeton University Press, 1977). Alfred Doren, *Le arti fiorentine,* 2 vols. (Florence: Le Monnier, 1940). John M. Najemy, *Corporatism and Consensus in Florentine Electoral Politics, 1280-1400* (Chapel Hill: University of North Carolina Press, 1982). Dale Kent, *The Rise of the Medici: Faction in Florence* (Oxford: Oxford University Press, 1978).

[36]Weissman, *Ritual Brotherhood.* Kent and Kent, *Neighbours and Neighbourhood.*

[37]Weissman, *Ritual Brotherhood.* Trexler, *Public Life.*

[38]Trexler, *Public Life,* 49.

honor of its inhabitants to devotion to the city's chief saints. In the Florentine feast of the Magi, the link between space, sacred charisma, and earthly honor was especially obvious. In this Medici-sponsored celebration of the fifteenth century, representatives of each of three quarters of Florence, dressed as Magi kings, paid homage to the fourth quarter, passing the Medici palace and walking on to "Bethlehem," the Medici-dominated convent of San Marco, to adore the Christ Child.[39] In contrast to Venice, private groups in Florence enhanced their charisma and their claims by manipulating sacred spaces. There the sacred was subject to the same particularist forces as was the secular. Among the constants of Florentine history are that every regime laid claim to legitimacy by employing the city's vocabulary of sacred space and that social ties to local places constrained the thoroughgoing expansion of public over private space.

Naples shows even more dramatically the strangely contradictory forces playing upon sacred objects and place names, which were ritually invoked by authorities for social control and adopted by intermittent rebels to legitimate themselves and to cleanse the body politic of evil rulers. One of the distinguishing features of Naples may have been that its central sacred object, the relic of Saint Janarius, recurrently stimulated prophetic enthusiasms through the prognostic capabilities of the triennial liquification of the saint's blood.[40] Since the liquifications only began after Saint Janarius's translation to Naples in 1497, the cult evolved during Naples' domination by foreign powers, principally Spain; and since social strife was manifest through struggles over the control of the cult, its socio-political role was ambiguous.[41]

Almost every year the archbishop, civic deputies, and the viceroy argued over rights of precedence in the ceremonies. For example, in 1646, the year before the revolution of Masaniello, the archbishop provocatively announced that the relics were his alone and denied the laity any rights to them. During the revolution the following year, the cathedral diarist assigned to describe the liquifications laconically recorded, "there is nothing to note because there was the revolution."[42] But the people saw visions of Saint Janarius and

---

[39]Ibid., 424-45

[40]Tommaso Costo, *Giunta di tre libri al compendio dell'Istoria del Regno di Napoli. Ne' quali si contiene quanto di notabile, e ad esso Regno appartenente e accaduto, dal principio dall'anno* MDLXIII *insino al fine dell'Ottantasei. Con la tavola delle cose memorabili, che in essa si contengono* (Venice: Gio. Battista Cappelli e Gioseffo Peluso, 1588), 120.

[41]G. B. Alfano and A. Amitrano, *Il miracolo di S. Gennaro in Napoli* (Naples: Scarpati, 1950), 145. Cf. Giuseppe Galasso, "Ideologia e sociologia del patronato di San Tommaso d'Aquino su Napoli (1605)," in *Per la storia sociale e religiosa del Mezzogiorno d'Italia,* ed. G. Galasso and Carla Russo, 2 vols. (Naples: Guida Editori, 1982). I wish to thank John Marino for bringing Galasso's article to my attention.

[42]Archivio dell'Arcivescovado, Naples (hereafter, AAN), MS titled "I diari dei ceremonieri della cattedrale di Napoli," 3: 165. Franco Strazzullo, *I diari dei cerimonieri della cattedrale di Napoli: Una fonte per la storia napoletana* (Naples: Agar, 1961), xxi.

employed his image on rebel coins, stealing his favor, in effect, from the archbishop, who was constrained from presiding over the regular liquification miracle. Additionally, a dark, miracle-working image of the Virgin offered special assistance to the poor of the fruit market; and on several occasions, while the authorities squabbled over the blood of Saint Janarius, her feast days supplied the occasions for piazza uprisings. In 1647, in fact, the market-place church of Santa Maria del Carmine served as the stage for Masaniello's raptured but short-lived revolutionary performance.[43] The great Neapolitan revolution consisted, in large part, of a competition among saints. After Masaniello's death, the archbishop interpreted a dramatically complete liquification as a sign of the saint's pleasure with the suppression of the rebellion: "In particular," reads the cathedral diary, "His Eminence commented more than once about never having seen [the blood] so beautifully [liquified], since after calamitous times [in the past] it had always appeared thus as a happy augury for our city . . . which has in the end been liberated from the tyranny of the mob."[44]

Even more than Florence's, Naples' sacred and political centers were widely dispersed; its cathedral housing the miraculous relics of Janarius lay far from the Castel Nuovo, where thick stone walls protected the viceroys. Large sections of the city were divided among the noble barons, and the packed popular quarters clustered around the marketplace where the Carmelites and other orders provided the spiritual services the parish clergy neglected. Unlike Venetian doges or the Medici of Florence, no Neapolitan authority succeeded in capturing for himself the charisma of Saint Janarius through the sacralization of urban spaces and institutions, a failure that assisted in keeping Naples permanently unstable and politically backward.

An even more extreme example of such a failure might be Udine, a city where social divisions had clear cultural and linguistic correlates. In the early sixteenth century Udine and the surrounding Friulan countryside witnessed some of the most widespread and violent revolts by artisans and peasants in Renaissance Italy. In 1511 more than twenty palaces in Udine were looted and burned and perhaps two dozen castles beseiged and damaged in the nearby countryside. What is most remarkable about these disturbances, especially when compared to the nearly contemporaneous revolts in the South Tyrol and Upper Swabia, is the absence of any religious content. Even the urban riots of Udine lacked the sensitivity to symbolic places so evident in similar disturbances in Florence and Naples.

---

[43]Burke, *Historical Anthropology*, 191-206. Rosario Villari, "Masaniello: Contemporary and Recent Interpretations," *Past and Present* 108 (1985): 117-32. Cf. Rothkrug, "Holy Shrines," 175-76.

[44]AAN, "I diari dei cerimonieri della cattedrale di Napoli," 2: 173.

This relative poverty of Christian imagery was widespread even though for nearly four centuries the region had been an ecclesiastical principality under the patriarchs of Aquileia and still had an exceptionally large establishment of religious, constituting nearly 4 percent of the population of Udine alone. But this establishment was notoriously neglectful of its pastoral duties. Even after Trent, suburban parish churches were still being used as barns, and the functioning of Udine's cathedral was jeopardized by a lack of liturgical vessels and ill repair. One report noted that the roof leaked so badly that divine offices might as well be said in the open. A visiting cardinal lamented that cathedral canons were infamous street fighters, most parish priests were illiterate and incapable of reciting the Mass, and the monasteries were dangerous places where the monks divided into armed camps. The cathedral chapter and the civil government were forever bickering over the administration of the divine cult, but artisans and suburban peasants were apparently indifferent to the expressive possibilities of religious ritual and sacred places, neither invoking the saints nor following a ritual geography during disturbances.[45] Their models of representation derived from other sources, the vendetta, factional loyalty, magic, and carnival practices, while the populace was far more open to Protestant doctrines than the Venetians, Florentines, or Neapolitans. The Cardinal of San Severina complained in 1535 that monasteries in Udine could barely survive from what charity trickled in from the laity because "this land is close to German places infested with Lutheran lies."[46] Lacking a charismatic center, the extremely agonistic society of Friuli was symbolically atomistic, failing to accept any social bodies larger than family and faction.

The gap between ecclesiastical institutions and popular spiritual life was so vast that the town remained in a semi-feudal, almost clannish environment in which animal totems and heraldic blazons carried greater emotive power than relics and images. Neighborhoods in Udine demarcated factional turfs, and even the images of the Virgin, erected about the city (probably in imitation of Venetian practice) seem to have been largely ignored by the laity. Much as did the Spanish viceroy of Naples, the Venetian *luogotenente* in Udine, who after 1420 was officially in charge, lived as the outsider he was, separated from the citizens on a strongly fortified hill within the city; the cathedral and monasteries, extensions of factional patronage systems, were thoroughly incapable of providing refuge from the recurrent strife.[47] Udine might not represent so much a failure of cognition or of faith as a failure of Christianity and of political institutions to create a civic culture by encouraging the veneration of images in public places.

[45]Battistella, "Udine nel secolo XVI," 1-17. The situation in Friuli paralleled the prince-bishoprics in Germany. Rothkrug, "German Holiness," 162.

[46]Battistella, "Udine nel secolo XVI," 7.

[47]These comments come from a book I am currently preparing on vendetta and factional strife in Friuli during the fifteenth and sixteenth centuries.

In all these cities, conflicting forces exerted pressure on the sacred. On the one hand, relations with the sacred presented an idealized pattern for human social relations that emphasized the virtues of hierarchy, deference, and obedience and that encouraged civic concord by investing urban places with a hallowed character. Ecclesiastic and secular authorities cooperated by representing the sacred in ways that would serve desirable social ends, but their effectiveness largely depended on the ability of the civil government to marshal support and suppress opposition. Although all governments appeared to legitimate themselves through divine sanction, only those regimes that built or forced some degree of social consensus succeeded in achieving legitimacy.

On the other hand, agonistic relations among individuals and urban groups – families, neighborhoods, guilds, classes – were projected onto the sacred, creating counter pressures that gave spiritual sanction to civil conflicts. In Venice the Virgin encouraged passivity; in Naples she sponsored rebellion. In all of these cities, sacred places and objects were approached and understood through public performances and rituals, but the meaning of gestures of reverence came not from the form of the performance itself but from what one might call the social script. In the theater states, the authorities made certain that they wrote the script and dominated the stage. The sincerity threshold was quite low because performing well brought rewards even if it masked crude self-interest and significant social conflict. In other cities, sacred performances were competitive – they constituted street fighting by another means – and the sincerity threshold was higher precisely because there was little agreement over the social script or even the most appropriate stage.

Where the sacred was most completely interwoven into the urban fabric, where the spiritual was most readily manifest in objects, where the incandescence of the holy could be found in the most mundane places, such as in Venice and Florence, one also finds the most effectively institutionalized, most politically sophisticated, the most economically advanced cities. Communities that failed to infuse urban spaces with a spiritual presence or to control their sacred objects were more awkwardly organized, more conflict-ridden, more economically backward, and perhaps more often open to religious reformist ideas. Such a pattern is, of course, the exact inverse of what traditional Durkheimian sociology might lead one to expect and differs, as well, from the more recent revisionist view that all societies are equally ritualized.[48] It is not the amount of ritual that counts but its character and its relationship to social behavior and verbal protestations.

The proper balance between ritual and the word, performance and intention, spirit and objects in representing the sacred was certainly one of the more vexing issues of the sixteenth century. Debated by theologians and

[48]Cf. the comments on this issue in Burke, *Historical Anthropology*, 223-24.

humanists, these issues met the hard realities of daily social life in the cities. When one recalls Luther's reaction to his Roman sojourn or Erasmus's complaints about the moral laxity among celebrants of the liturgy and lay believers alike, one wonders how much of the Reformation may have come from misunderstandings of the various dialects of popular devotion, misunderstandings that were stumblings, in effect, upon the threshold of sincerity.

II

Learned Culture

Die Gelehrten die Verkehrten:
Popular Response to Learned Culture in the Renaissance and Reformation

Heiko A. Oberman

Isti sunt subversores pietatis, derisores simplicium, deceptores vulgi.
From a letter by Geert Groote to
William of Salvarvilla, early 1379.

. . . . du soltt inen nit glauben, so sie sprechen:
ja, die bawrenn verstehen die sach nit.
Meint ich doch, weil die verkerrten gelerrten die Schrifft
verstünden, sie würden am ersten Selig.
Eynn Dialogus ader gesprech. . .
(Erfurt 1523), fol. a ii b; b ii a

"THE REFORMATION WAS MADE not just by many individuals holding a common belief, but by collective forms of behavior."[1] I regard this statement by Bob Scribner as a fine formulation of the advance made in Reformation scholarship over the last twenty years. The formulation would be cleaner and less subject to misinterpretation if it had said explicitly that the Reformation was made not just by many individuals holding a common belief, but also by collective forms of behavior. The finely honed balance and true duality in this vision is a high ideal,[2] behind which actual scholarship in the field of sixteenth-century studies has fallen consistently.

Die Gelehrten die Verkehrten

Admittedly, the theory of economic causation is no longer held up as the sole factor determining communal behavior, except in Western – especially West German – caricatures of the Marxist contribution to the

---

[1]Robert Scribner, "Is There a Social History of the Reformation?" *Social History* 4 (1976): 483-505; 501.

[2]A significant theoretical clarification is provided by the Chicago School of Sociology (Interactionism) as interpreted by Ronald F. E. Weissman: "The primary unit of analysis is the social relation linking individuals, for it is individual interaction that mediates or underlies what is perceived as group interaction or group identity." Here quoted from "Reconstructing Renaissance Sociology: The 'Chicago School' and the study of Renaissance Society," in *Persons in Groups: Social Behavior as Identity Formation in Medieval and Renaissance Europe*, ed. R. Trexler (Binghamton, N.Y.: Medieval & Renaissance Texts and Studies, 1985), 39-46; 41. Weissman's point of departure applies obviously to the Middle Ages and the Reformation as well: "What Renaissance sociology requires is a more pragmatic, Nominalist approach to the study of society." Ibid., 40. The same balance can be noted in the work of the Sorbonne medievalist, Bernard Guenée, "directeur d'Études" at the E.P.H.E. For him, the analysis of structures is "irremplaçable": "Elle éclairat le passé d'une merveilleuse cohérence. Mais elle le rendait trop simple . . . . L'étude des structures me semblait aussi donner une place trop large à la nécessité." *Entre l'Église et l'État* (Paris: Galimard, 1987), 13f.

history of the transition from a late feudal to an early capitalist society. But the primacy of social history over intellectual history is the seldom voiced, yet virulent presupposition of much of the best work done in our field today. Insofar as the emphasis on communal groups still tolerates the study of individual agents, their intellectual or, as the case may be, religious motivation is all too often privatized. The widespread but equally anachronistic use of the loaded French word *politiques* tends to suggest that such private convictions did not allow these agents to escape from the "scientific law" that history is the story of the struggle for gain: for prowess, power, and prosperity.

Against this stubborn tendency to slight the evidence that we are dealing with an epoch when reform always comprised individual *and* communal, religious *and* social renewal, the dialectic between social and intellectual history offers the integrating analytical principle which enables us to rise above both determinism and elitism – to use the two terms which the opposing parties prefer in describing each other.

The most concise expression of both the division of labor and the common goal is, it seems to me, as follows: *conditions of life* (I take this to comprise *Strukturgeschichte* and *Ereignisgeschichte*, that is, economic, demographic, geographic, dietary data in the narrowest sense of the word, as well as crises, such as famine, war, and social disorder) *only become historical factors shaping a communal mentality when recorded, evaluated, and advanced by intellectual leaders.* This formulation has a double critical edge: first, it insists, against traditional intellectual history, that ideas are never sufficiently grasped when the study of treatises and documents is not extended to the analysis of their social matrix and their societal impact. The edge against traditional social history is that the study of matrix and impact cannot be short-circuited, but must bow to the iron rule of the sequence of conditions-program-impact.[3] This sequence requires that central attention be given to intellectual history in order to understand both spokesmen and leaders.

Thomas A. Brady, Jr., concluded his fine essay on the state and task of social history in Steven Ozment's *Reformation Europe: A Guide to Research* with a programmatic thesis: "Neither confessional nor racial/cultural explanations of the place of the Reformation in European history have survived the fire of historical criticism. Perhaps the social-historical explanation will."[4] I do not see how this can or should come about unless social history is prepared to respect and pursue this three-stage procedure: conditions-program-impact.

[3]Robert M. Kingdon, *Geneva and the Coming of the Wars of Religion in France: 1555-1563* (Geneva: Droz, 1956), 128, illuminated this interaction with the felicitous phrase "social smoldering" when he expressed his interest "in the process by which ideological leadership may assist social smoldering toward explosion."

[4]Steven Ozment, *Reformation Europe: A Guide to Research* (St. Louis: Center for Reformation Research, 1982), 161-81; 176.

If the foregoing might still seem to be an exercise in abstractions, we now turn to an area closer to our daily battleground. The popular broadsides against so-called "Whig history" tend to slay both the deserving and the undeserving. They tend to separate – indeed, divorce – literate, elite culture from an illiterate, popular culture. Thus, I understand Rodney Hilton's disdain for the earlier interpreters of "the English peasantry in the later Middle Ages":[5] their fatal error appears to be that they relied on the witness of spokesmen for the upper levels of society. And thus I understand the hesitation of Bob Scribner to accept my analysis of the German Peasants' War as "basically a religious movement" because it drew on the evidence of eyewitnesses belonging to the cultured elite.[6] This also, I surmise, is a basic factor in the warm reception which Carlo Ginzburg received for *The Cheese and the Worms*. After all, he presents the not-so-simple miller, Menocchio (1532-c.1600), as the non-elite representative of a silent majority and recipient of an "ancient oral tradition," yet sufficiently literate to allow Ginzburg to explore an otherwise unknown "substratum of peasant beliefs."[7]

By insisting on the crucial role of the so-called "cultured elite," we do not underrate the "common man"[8] or reduce him to mere passivity in the communication process. A trend in this direction is not to be ignored. A case in point is the important and stimulating monograph of Bob Scribner, *For the Sake of Simple Folk*. His point of departure is sound and convincing: "Printing was, in fact, an addition to, not a replacement for, oral communication."[9] But in concentrating on the pamphlet literature as "propaganda," Scribner is increasingly more fascinated by the pamphlet as the means to *shape* popular culture – and thus create a new "symbolic world" – than by the extent to which it *reflects* popular culture. Bernd Moeller's insistence on the primacy of the sermon over the pamphlet as decisive medium is, however justified, in this respect no real advance.[10]

[5]R. H. Hilton, *The English Peasantry in the Later Middle Ages* (Oxford: Clarendon, 1975), 9ff.

[6]Heiko A. Oberman, *The Dawn of the Reformation* (Edinburgh: T. & T. Clark, 1986), 155-78; 172. Cf. Robert Scribner, "Is There a Social History of the Reformation?" 494 n. 29.

[7]Carlo Ginzburg, *The Cheese and the Worms: The Cosmos of a Sixteenth-Century Miller*, trans. John and Anne Tedeschi (Baltimore: Johns Hopkins University Press, 1980), xxii, 20-21, 51, 59, 71.

[8]See n. 15 below; cf. n. 26 below.

[9]Robert Scribner, *For the Sake of Simple Folk: Popular Propaganda for the German Reformation* (Cambridge: Cambridge University Press, 1981), 2.

[10]See Bernd Moeller's review in *Historische Zeitschrift* 237 (1983): 707-10. For the preceding stage in this discussion, see Robert Scribner, "How Many Could Read? Comments on Bernd Moeller's 'Stadt und Buch'" in *Stadtbürgertum und Adel in der Reformation: Studien zur Sozial-geschichte der Reformation in England und Deutschland*, Veröffentlichungen des Deutschen Historischen Instituts London, Bd. 5, ed. W. J. Mommsen, et al. (Stuttgart: Klett-Cotta, 1979), 44-45.

I share Ginzburg's hypothesis of the two-way permeation of high and low culture, but regard his timetable for its termination (1525/35) and his assumption of an ensuing one-sided "indoctrination from above" as untenable.[11] Divested of modern sentiments, indoctrination has always been the goal of the pursuit of knowledge. Throughout the Middle Ages, "pure" research was just as far removed from the mind of the most abstract scholastic master as from the soul of the mystic most devoted to the "vita contemplativa."

In the following, I will be concerned with how "learned culture," if considered as a separate universe of communication and in this sense as an elitist "textual community," could have such a popular impact that (as we all seem to agree) literacy developed and grew by leaps and bounds. In concentrating on one revealing and hitherto unexplored source, it is my intent to show that in the later Middle Ages, notwithstanding deep-rooted suspicion of scholars, scholarship, and scholarly institutions, an equally deep-rooted and socially broad-based confidence can be discerned – a confidence in true learning and in its crucial contribution to church and society.[12]

The title chosen for this section is one of the best known slogans of sixteenth-century pamphlet literature. The phrase "Die Gelehrten die Verkehrten"[13] has the attraction of rhyme, just as easily memorable as *Affen* and *Pfaffen*. Both proved to be powerful weapons in the heyday of the spread of pamphlet literature in the service of the Reformation – broadly speaking, in the decade from 1515 through 1525. Afterwards, this form of indoctrination tapered off noticeably, probably under the impact of the

---

[11]Cf. Ginzburg, *The Cheese and the Worms*, 126. "Thus there is a symptomatic value in a limited case such as Menocchio's. It forcefully poses a problem the significance of which is only now beginning to be recognized: that of the popular roots of a considerable part of high European culture, both medieval and post-medieval. Such figures as Rabelais and Breughel probably were not unusual exceptions. All the same, they closed an era characterized by hidden but fruitful exchanges, moving in both directions between high and popular cultures. The subsequent period was marked, instead, by an increasingly rigid distinction between the culture of the dominant classes and the artisan and peasant cultures, as well as by the indoctrination of the masses from above. We can place the break between these two periods in the second half of the sixteenth century, basically coinciding with the intensification of social differentiation under the impulse of the price revolution. But the decisive crisis had occurred a few decades earlier, with the Peasants' War and the reign of the Anabaptists in Münster."

[12]This corresponds with the confidence of a reformer like Luther to collect "popular" aphorisms as nuggets of wisdom. See my article "Stadtreformation und Fürstenreformation," in *Humanismus und Reformation als kulturelle Kräfte in der deutschen Geschichte*, ed. Lewis W. Spitz (Berlin: De Gruyter, 1981), 80-103; 81-82.

[13]See Ernst Thiele, ed., *Luthers Sprichwörtersammlung* (Weimar: H. Böhlaus Nachfolger, 1900), 33f. *Johann Kesslers Sabbata*, ed. Historischer Verein des Kantons St. Gallen (St. Gallen: Fehr'sche Buchhandlung, 1902) 537. E. Hampel, "Fischarts Anteil an dem Gedicht: 'Die Gelehrten – die Verkehrten.'" *Programm des Realgymnasiums zu Naumburg*, 1903. Quoted by Otto Clemen, *Flugschriften aus den ersten Jahren der Reformation*, 4 vols. (Nieuwkoop: De Graaf, 1967; reprint of ed. Halle, 1907-11), 1: 48 n. 20.

criminalization of what the authorities called the *schlechten Prediger,* who lost their livlihoods or lives in the aftermath of the peasants' revolt.[14]

This slogan, invented to discredit the proud claims of the "ivory tower," was put in the mouth of peasant and burgher in order to eradicate by ridicule the authority of the medieval doctors in general, but its sarcasm reached a notably shrill tone when pitched against the monks. They should have been responsible for the education of the masses but, as Eberlin of Günzburg († 1533) put it: ". . . itel schul thandt halten sie dem schleckten volck für . . . . Es ist ein arm ding, das so grosse eslische unwissenheit regiert in den klösteren."[15] If one wishes to retain something of the original alliteration and sentiment, one should translate "Die Gelehrten die Verkehrten" as "those dangerous deviant doctors – they stray and 'stroy."[16]

Though we know far less than hitherto assumed about the social distribution of the readers of pamphlet literature and the number of re-editions, a conservative estimate of numbers sold – between 1501 and 1530 approximately ten million copies, or just under one copy per capita for the Empire[17] – suffices to confirm the traditional German identification of the broadsheets as *Sturmtruppen der Reformation,* the avant-garde indoctrination of the populace with a new "symbolic world." And yet, there is another dimension: the pamphlets allow us glimpses at widely spread reform aspirations. By carefully listing the concatenation of arguments and clusters of biblical quotations, one can observe that by the end of 1523 the pamphlets had succeeded in establishing a common market of *gravamina* through "swap and exchange" between locally and territorially active literary circles which apparently formed social networks as *sodalitates* in the cities and *confraternitates* around the monasteries. At the same time, the early pamphlets

---

[14]See the revealing record of the prosecution of "Peasant-Preachers" drawn up by Justus Maurer, *Prediger im Bauernkrieg* (Stuttgart: Calwer Verlag, 1979), esp. 247ff.

[15]Johann Eberlin von Günzburg, *XV Bundsgenossen* s. 1, s. a (Basel, 1521), ed. Ludwig Enders, (Halle a.S. 1896), *VI. Bundsgenoß* 58; 60. It should be noted that Eberlin – just as Luther – used "common man," here and throughout, not for "poor people" (or "peasants"!), but for the *simplices,* the "uninformed" or, more often, the "ill-informed laity"! I am following his usage.

[16]This critique is here not directed against the monastery as an institution, but against its deformation and devaluation: what "jetz kleine kind wissen, können alte männer in klösteren nit, so doch etwan [!] grosse kunst in der kutten was." *VI. Bundsgenoß, 58; 60.*

[17]See the timeline suggested by Hans Joachim Köhler, "Erste Schritte zu einem Meinungsprofil der frühen Reformationszeit," in *Martin Luther: Probleme seiner Zeit,* ed. Volker Press and Dieter Stievermann (Stuttgart: Klett-Cotta, 1986), 244-81; 270. Cf. "Die Flugschriften: Versuch der Präzisierung eines geläufigen Begriffs," in *Festgabe für Ernst Walter Zeeden,* ed. Horst Rabe, Hansgeorg Molitor, and Hans-Christoph Rublack (Münster: Aschendorff, 1976), 36-61; 43.

had an impact reaching far beyond these "textual communities"[18] because they not only conveyed but also confirmed what was alive and fermenting in a much broader illiterate social layer. Just like the sermons, the pamphlets created their own audience; but far more than the sermons, the pamphlets played to an already existing gallery. By focusing on the Modern Devotion as one vocal section in this gallery, it is possible to shed new light both on the movement itself and on popular aspirations on the eve of the Reformation.

The Program of the Devotio Moderna

When we now turn our attention to the Modern Devotion, we discover that its chief tenet is the pursuit of the true monastic vision of Saint Bernard, Saint Francis, and Saint Bonaventura. Yet in a new "secular" key, its most revealing slogan is the loaded phrase "purus Christianus, verus monachus," reflected – I am convinced – in the telling adage of the early Erasmus, written at the time of his *Enchiridion* (1501): "monachatus non est pietas."[19] Its cutting programmatic edge is immediately evident when placed against the background of the claim that only the monastic vows are the sure road to

---

[18]Cf. the important extension of this term advocated by Brian Stock, *The Implications of Literacy: Written Language and Models of Interpretation in the Eleventh and Twelfth Centuries* (Princeton: Princeton University Press, 1983), 9ff., 90-91., 405-6. A constitutive factor for each "textual community" is the search for legitimation of change (reform). With reference to the movements associated with the so-called "Peasants' War," this is highlighted in the theoretically significant article of Wilfried Schulze, "Soziale Bewegungen als Phänomen des 16. Jahrhunderts," in *Säkulare Aspekte der Reformationszeit,* ed. Heinz Angermeier (Munich: Oldenbourg, 1983), 113-30; 129-30.

[19]Desiderius Erasmus, *Opus Epistolarum,* ed. P. S. Allen, 12 vols. (Oxford: Clarendon, 1906-58), 1:374:28 (no. 164), quoted by Eugene F. Rice, Jr., *Saint Jerome in the Renaissance* (Baltimore: Johns Hopkins University Press, 1985), 133. The most revealing "Brethren statement" is the preceding clause: ". . . perinde quasi extra cucullum Christianismus non sit," ll. 24-25. On this point I differ from the excellent biography of Erasmus by Cornelis Augustijn, *Erasmus von Rotterdam: Leben, Werk, Wirkung* (Munich: Beck, 1986) (Dutch original, Baarn, 1986), 51-52: "Im Kreise der Devotio moderna . . . konnte man mit diesen Worten nichts anfangen."

By pursuing the "trail of St. Jerome," Eugene Rice noticed that Erasmus was "especially irritated by religious who claimed that Jerome had founded their order." *Saint Jerome,* 133. In Gabriel Biel's defense of the *Devotio Moderna* (c. 1470), we find the general critique of the proud appeal to founding father in his terse retort: we seek perfection "sub uno abbate Christo Jhesu. . . ." See my *Masters of the Reformation* (Cambridge: Cambridge University Press, 1981), 54. Some fifty years earlier, Derk of Herxen (near Zwolle) explicitly rejected the claim of the Dominican Grabow that St. Jerome set the standard of the true monastic life. See Willem Lourdaux, "Dirk of Herxen's tract 'De Utilitate Monachorum'": A Defence of the Lifestyle of the Brethren and Sisters of the Common LIfe," in *Bijdragen: Tijdschrift voor filosofie en theologie* 33 (1972): 412-36. Yet, just as Erasmus held Jerome in the highest regard as biblical exegete, the Brethren were eager to associate their name with his: the House in Delft was called St. Hieronymusdal, the Latin School in Utrecht was named after him.

the *vita perfecta,* or when contrasted with the official teaching that the vows provide "the monopoly on the perfect life."[20]

Even six hundred years after the founding of the Windesheim Congregation in 1387, one serious weakness in the presentation of the Modern Devotion still prevails: that the establishment of the Windesheim Congregation was an unfortunate deviation from the original vision of Geert Groote. But also in this clerical branch the view has never been questioned that the whole movement issuing from Geert Groote represents the *status medius* between the monastery and the world. Even in Gabriel Biel's *De communi vita* (c. 1480), Groote's insistence on the common life as the crucial alternative to the cloistered life is clearly articulated: "religion" should not be understood as "the monastic life," but as Christian faith![21] For all three branches – the Sisters, the Brethren, and the Canons Regular of the Windesheim congregation – the true Christian is the true monk: *purus Christianus, verus monachus.*

The most recent literature[22] shows that a major advance has been made through the clarification of the legal status of the movement as *medius status* between the *saeculares saeculariter viventes* and the *status religiosorum.* This advance, however, has not yet been recognized as the breakthrough it really is. The Modern Devotion was apparently not just a local Dutch movement, but the tip of the iceberg of late medieval organized lay piety, reaching from communities of virgins and widows, and from *Hospitalbrüdern* and *Bußbrüdern* to the members of fraternities and confraternities. This *medius status* of lay religiosity was, in the words of Kaspar Elm, "für die Zeitgenossen (jedoch) mindestens so wichtig, wie das seit Jahrhunderten mit größerem Nachdruck erforschte Ordenswesen."[23]

---

[20]See Kaspar Elm in the best available orientation about the present state of research, "Die Bruderschaft von Gemeinsamen Leben" *Ons Geestelijk Erf* 59 (1985): 470ff. In a more general sense, see W. Lourdaux, "De Broeders van het Gemene Leven," *Bijdragen: Tijdschrift voor filosofie en theologie* 33 (1972): 372-416; 397.

[21]Cf. my discussion in *The Harvest of Medieval Theology: Gabriel Biel and Late Medieval Nominalism,* 3d ed. (Cambridge, Mass.: Harvard University Press, 1981; 1st ed., 1963), 14ff.; and in *Werden und Wertung der Reformation: Vom Wegestreit zum Glaubenskampf,* 3d ed. (Tübingen: Mohr, 1980; 1st ed, 1977), 8-9; (English version, *Masters of the Reformation*).

[22]Reaching from the congress volumes, *Moderne Devotie: Figuren en Facetten* [Nijmegen, 1984] and *Geert Grote en Moderne Devotie* (Nijmegen Congress, 1984), ed. J. Andriessen, P. Bange, A. G. Weiler, [*Ons Geestelijk Erf* 59 (1985): 113-505] (Nijmegen, 1985), to G. H. Gerrits' study of Gerard Zerbolt of Zutphen, *Inter Timorem et Spem: A Study of the Theological Thought of Gerard Zerbolt of Zutphen (1367-1398),* SMRTh 37 (Leiden: Brill, 1986), and to the rich English anthology edited by John Van Engen, *The Brothers and Sisters of the Modern Devotion* (New York: Paulist Press, 1987). For earlier literature, see W. Jappe Alberts, "Zur Historiographie der Devotio Moderna und ihrer Erforschung," *Westfälische Forschungen* 2 (1958): 51-67. For the history and impact of the Windesheim Congregation, see the preciously precise and encompassing three-volume work of J.G.R. Acquoy, *Het Klooster Windesheim en zijn Invloed* (Utrecht: Gebr. Van der Post, 1875-80).

[23]Kaspar Elm, "Die Bruderschaft von Gemeinsamen Leben," 476.

For the first time, we start to get in our historical sights an initially loosely tied association of lay organizations which managed first to survive and then to gain in social status, notwithstanding the constant climate of suspicion and restraining tactics promoted by the established orders, particularly the Dominicans. The sharp accusation of heresy by Matthew Grabow, O.P. during the final days of the Council of Constance had the opposite effect when his defamation of Devotio Moderna was countered (3 April 1418) by no one less than the "Church Father of the later Middle Ages," Johannes Gerson.[24] The charge that the Sisters and Brethren were really a cover organization for Beghards and Beguines helped instead to raise the latter's status.

Bernd Moeller, in his sketch of late medieval piety, concluded from the decrease in heresy cases during the fifteenth century that heresy itself apparently (*offenbar!*) disappeared "weil der Ausbruch aus dem kirchlichen System seine frühere Attraktion verloren hatte."[25] This conclusion is an optical illusion due to a too narrow theological understanding of both Church and heresy. Suspicion of heresy is not directed at "Ausbruch" but at "Umbruch" – in the fourteenth as much as in the fifteenth century. The Devotio Moderna, speaking for a much broader movement of voluntary lay associations, never intended to "break out of the Church," but piously enlarged its boundaries by irreverently redefining its nucleus, the monastic life. Particularly the records of the Dutch Sisterhouses are replete with references to investigations and accusations by inquisitors who succeeded in forcing several communities to join the Franciscan Tertiaries; obviously their "irreverence" was interpreted as trespassing the critical borderline to heresy.

On the eve of the Reformation, the carriers of the New Devotion not only had achieved far more than a foothold in late medieval society, but also had learned to endure and counter the attacks of the monastic elite. To be fair, particularly the mendicants – often contrasted with the "good monks," the Carthusians – had been assiduously assailed. At the beginning stood the charge of Geert Groote, early in 1379, ranking them with the Pharisees and the lawyers: "Ubi pietas, ubi religio?"! Groote had not hesitated to throw a three-fold curse on the mendicants' preaching as the source of all heresy and as the poison killing piety in all of Europe: "terrena, animalis, diabolica." And again, it had been Groote who had not minced words, speaking for the sake of common man: "Isti sunt subversores pietatis, derisores simplicium,

---

[24]For Grabow's "conclusiones," see Joannes Gerson, *Opera omnia*, 5 vols., ed. Lud. Ellies Du Pin (Antwerp, 1706), cols. 470-74. Gerson's defense in Gerson, *Oeuvres*, ed. Palémon Glorieux, 10: 70-72.

[25]"Deutschland im Zeitalter der Reformation," in *Deutsche Geschichte*, ed. B. Moeller, M. Heckel, R. Vierhaus, K. O. von Aretin, Vol 2, *Frühe Neuzeit* (Göttingen: Vandenhoeck & Ruprecht, 1985), 26.

deceptores vulgi."[26] Here we find nothing less than the Latin version of the accusation that "they stray and 'stroy." The slogan "Die Gelehrten die Verkehrten" is not a novel weapon in the arsenal of Reformation propaganda, but is the exact formulation of a conviction hardened by a century of repression and cow(l)towing. Once again, we are alerted to the fact that the pamphlets of the sixteenth century not only shaped but also reflected what might be called public opinion.[27]

The Pursuit of Holiness

It is still widely assumed that the Modern Devotion was not only an anti-scholastic but also an anti-intellectual movement.[28] Upon closer scrutiny, this traditional evaluation strongly relies on trends in fourteenth-century sources; that is, on the seminal works of the founding fathers Geert Groote († 1384), Gerard Zerbolt of Zutphen († 1398), and Florens Radewijns († 1400). And, admittedly, there is some justification for the characterization of any movement in terms of its *initia*. Yet, by the time the Devotio Moderna is confronted with Renaissance and Reformation, it is some 130 to 150 years after the founding period.

Hence we have to ask a new question: what characteristics survived or surfaced in the latter part of the fifteenth century? By that time, the third – clerical – branch of the movement had reached not only Paris in the West, but also Württemberg in the South, where Gabriel Biel († 1495) and Wendelin Steinbach († 1519) were outspoken representatives of the movement, both of them university professors, both of them without a trace of anti-intellectualism. Insofar as it can be argued that the truly popular impact of the movement can be seen in the lay branches of the Brethren and Sisters of the Common Life, we must turn to the widely dispersed writings of later generations to perceive the shift in self-understanding visible in the

---

[26]Letter to his Parisian friend and mentor, William of Salvarvilla, dated early 1379. *Gerardi Magni Epistolae*, ed. Willelmus Mulder (Antwerp: Sumptibus Societatis Editricis Neerlandiae, 1933), 27. "Hic pharizei, iuriste et religiosi. . .; hic sunt qui suas iusticias faciunt, Dei iustitiam ignorantes" (28). "Deus, Deus, quale mixtum ex cortice et nuce scripturarum et ex cantu Syrenarum suboritur! Hinc perfidie contra Deum et veritatem, omnem Europeam capientes, hinc hereses, hinc philosophia, nam philosophia, secundum Jeronimum [PL 22, 667] mater et nutrix heresium" (29-30). Here we touch on the heart of Groote's "anti-intellectualism": the simple folk cannot understand you – in the end, you preach only to the clergy; "Quid restat ut solis clericis predicetis. . ." and few among them! (32).

[27]See my article, "Zwischen Agitation und Reformation: Die Flugschriften als 'Judenspiegel,'" in *Flugschriften als Massenmedium der Reformationszeit*, ed. Hans-Joachim Köhler (Stuttgart: Klett-Cotta, 1981), 269-89.; 287-88. Cf. "Stadtreformation und Fürstenreformation," in *Humanismus und Reformation als kulturelle Kräfte in der deutschen Geschichte*, ed. Lewis W. Spitz (Berlin: De Gruyter, 1981), 80-103; 81-82.

[28]An exception has to be made for the corrections of R. R. Post, *Modern Devotion*, offered by G. Codina Mir, *Aux sources de la pédagogie des Jésuites: Le "modus Parisiensis"* (Rome: Institutum Historicum Societatis Iesu, 1968), esp. 160ff.; and W. Lourdaux, "De Broeders van het Gemene Leven," 397.

anecdotes (*exempla*) they used to memorialize the founding fathers in chronicles best subsumed under the general title *De viris illustribus*.

After the middle of the fifteenth century, we notice a true eruption of such pious portrayals,[29] which as a genre continued the original *rapiaria* for meditation.[30] They are inspiring recollections from "our own" religious tradition, something like a *Legenda Aurea* of the Modern Devotion. One such excerpt from a devotional *vitae-fratrum*, to be dated about 1480, compiled by an anonymous author, clearly belongs to the orbit of Deventer and Zwolle. It deserves our particular attention because of the peculiar way in which it touches upon our quest for the popular impact of learning. The title is really a brief table of contents: "Here follow some excerpts from the lives of our Founding Fathers, proffering proper material for our *collationes* at noon and at eventide."[31]

The text is unique in that it combines the typical theme of the *devoti*, namely, the pursuit of holiness – or in their own terminonolgy, the *reformacio virium*[32] – with virtuous scenes from the lives of the founding fathers of the

[29]See, e.g., the Chronicle of Mount St. Agnes, written by Thomas of Kempen († 1471) but continued through 1477. Available in English: *The Chronicle of the Canons Regular of Mount St. Agnes Written by Thomas à Kempis*, trans. J. P. Arthur (London: Kegan Paul, Trench, Trübner, 1906). Cf. Hubert Jedin's perceptive article "Thomas von Kempen als Biograph und Chronist," in his volume of collected essays, *Kirche des Glaubens, Kirche der Geschichte* 2 vols. (Freiburg: Herder, 1966), 1: 49-58. In the combination of three characteristic elements – conversio, humilitas, and apostolatus – Jedin finds the justification "die Devotio Moderna als Vorstufe der Katholischen Reform anzugliedern. . . " (58).

[30]Petronella Bange, *Spiegels der Christenen: Zelfreflectie en ideaalbeeld in laatmiddeleeuwse moralistisch-didactische traktaten* (Nijmegen, 1986), has delineated an important second devout didactic genre, also feeding into the *Collationes*. For her cautious analysis of the readership of these *Specula*, see 229-32.

[31]"Hic aliqua sequuntur ex vitis fratrum nostrorum prout materie convenit collationum nostrarum meridianarum et serotinarum." Museum Wasserburg, Anhold (Cleve). Primarily drawn up on the basis of the *Scriptum* of Rudolph Dier of Muiden: (Rudolph Dier de Muden, *Scriptum de Magistro Gerardo Grote, Domino Florencia et aliis devotis Fratribus*, published by G. Dumbar in *Reipublicae Daventriensis ab Actis Analecta, seu vetera aliquot scripta inedita* 3 vols. [Deventer, 1719-25]: 2: 1-87), and the *Continuatio Scripti Rudolphi Dier de Muiden* by Petrus Hoorn (G. Dumbar, *Analecta* 1 [1719]: 88ff.). For a full transcription of this precious source, I am indebted to John Van Engen, who is preparing its publication in *Revue Bénédictine* 98 (1988). The Dutch version of many of the same portrayals in the Frensweger Manuscript of 1494 (UB Utrecht, Hs 8 L. 16) is edited and carefully annotated by W. J. Alberts and A. L. Hulshoff (Groningen, 1958). I shall refer to it as *FH*.

[32]In the context of this present investigation, we cannot develop the complex theme of the characteristics of the "devotion" typical of this pursuit of holiness. Striking is the major role of *timor Dei*, in the Dutch chronicles usually rendered not as "vrees" but as "anxt" or "angstlichheyt," a mood probably best captured as "pious anxiety." According to both biographers of Geert Groote – Thomas à Kempis († 1471) and Petrus Hoorn († 1479) – this was already so dominant with the founder, Groote, that he often abstained from communion:

Modern Devotion. This "proper" material was intended for the so-called *collationes*, a typical institution of the Modern Devotion,[33] a kind of revival meeting, organized twice a day for the members, open to the townspeople but particularly directed at the young students of the city schools placed under the pastoral care of the Brethren and Sisters.

The "historical" or – as the case may be – hagiographical scenes are organized under the headings of major virtues. Without structuring the evidence, I am now first going to report the entries that pertain to our theme:

DE STUDIO. Under the heading "De studio," Geert Groote, explicitly introduced with his academic title, *Magister,* liked to make a quick pizza (*pisa*) – contrary to Italian lore, apparently a typical Dutch dish![34] – so that he had more time for his studies: liberius vacaret studio (1.31f.).

DE ORACIONE. Under the heading "De Oracione" it was recalled that Rudolph – Rudolph Dier of Muiden (1384-1459) – could always, except

---

". . . sumeret corpus Salvatoris, quatenus saepe eum spiritualiter manducaret quem sacramentaliter sumere frequentius formidabat." Petrus Hoorn, *De vita magistri Gerardi Magni,* ed. W. J. Kühler, *Nederlands Archief voor Kerkgeschiedenis* 6 (1909): 325-70; 359. See Thomas à Kempis, *Vita Gerardi Magni,* ed. M. I. Pohl, in *Opera Omnia,* 7 (Freiburg i. B., 1922): 31-115; 63-64. Cf. *Scriptum,* ed. G. Dumbar, *Analecta* 1 (Deventer, 1719): 4. Stephanus Axters, *Geschiedenis van de Vroomheid in de Nederlanden,* 3: *De Moderne Devotie,* 4 vols. (Antwerp: De Sikkel, 1950-60), 55, has noted this anxiety (rendered by him more innocently as "schroom") and finds here the explanation for the hesitation among many of Geert's disciples to seek ordination. The text quoted is far more revealing, however, than expressing anxiety as such. Whereas the distinction between partaking (*sumere corpus*) *sacramentaliter* and *spiritualiter* is traditional church doctrine (see my *Dawn of the Reformation,* 243-44), the suggested sufficiency of the spiritual eating is the missing link with the famous "Letter of Hoen" (1524). Derived from the library of Wessel Gansfort, who was closely associated with the Brethren in Groningen, Hoen's letter was spurned by Luther, but praised by Zwingli as the key for the interpretation of *est* as "significat" in the words of institution, "Hoc est Corpus meum." See Cornelis Hoen, "Epistola christiana," in *Huldreich Zwinglis sämtliche Werke,* ed. Emil Egli, et al., 14 vols. (Berlin: C. A. Schwetschke und Sohn, 1905-59), 4: 512, 21-22. (The letter was carried by two Dutchmen, Johan Rodius and Georg Saganus, who met with Zwingli probably in the late summer 1524. See Walther Köhler, *Zwingli und Luther,* 2 vols. [Leipzig: Heinsius Nachfolger, 1923-54], 1:61-62.) All this is by now well known, as well as that there are some significant differences between the interpretations of Hoen and Zwingli, as there are also between those of Gansfort and Geert Groote. A new line of investigation is opened up, however, by "the missing link" of the psychological factor in the development of a scholastic distinction to an alternative in the *praxis pietatis*: the religious experience of "anxiety."

For a discussion of recent literature on the theme of anxiety in the later Middle Ages, see Dennis D. Martin, "Popular and Monastic Pastoral Issues in the Later Middle Ages," *Church History* 56 (1987): 320-332; 321-22. Vis-à-vis the trend to see the Reformation as the answer to the anxiety spawned by the teaching and sacraments of the "official" late medieval Church, it is to be noted that church-critical reform movements did not oppose but intensified this state of mind.

[33]The *collatio,* usually after the evening meal and for members of the house only, was a general monastic institution. It can be traced back to the *Regula Benedicti,* chap. 42, which refers to the *Collationes* of the "Father of all Monks," John Cassian. See *Patrologia Latina,* 49-50.

[34]Far less appetizing, but unfortunately more convincing, is the assumption that the Dutch concoction might have been pea soup. See Theodore van Zijl, *Gerard Groote: Ascetic and Reformer (1340-1384)* (Washington, D.C.: Catholic University of America Press, 1963), 130.

when he sat at his desk to write, be found on his knees, since in accordance
with the advice of Saint Francis he prayed more than he read. Rudolph liked
to quote the word of some Father: primo devoti, secundo scientifici, tertio
dissoluti (people are first devout, then become scholars, and hence go to pot)
(1.43-44). It is to be noted, however, that "scholars" are here referred to as
scientifici, perhaps best rendered as "knowledge freaks" or "eggheads." But
the meaning is clear: we have here in Latin the psycho/historical explanation
for the satire of the pamphlets, *Die Gelehrten, die Verkehrten.*

DE LABORE. Under the heading "De labore," a Dutch colleague of the
Italian Menocchio is introduced, namely the miller Matthias, who is highly
praised for the fact that whenever his manifold tasks allowed, he loved to
be studying on holy days "dans se lecioni et meditacioni . . ." (1.114-15).[35]
Brother Petrus Hoorn († 1479) is presented as a man who was so dedicated
to the high duty of writing, in this case transcription (*opus scripture*), that
even in the winter he would continue to pen his lines till the freezing cold
made him drop the quill from his stiff fingers – never allowing food or sleep
to interfere with his duties as *scriptor*, a task which he executed till his death
(1.132-38). Petrus rather sat behind his desk to write under the worst of
circumstances. He never desired a higher office in the liturgy or rule of the
house ("nunquam ad alia se officia facienda ordinari postulat"), but wanted
to remain a scriptor till his death. He was willing to make only one exception:
for delivering regular homilies to the school boys (*scolares*, 1.202) in public
and private sessions. If Brother Petrus would have died a hundred years later
as a Protestant, he would undoubtedly serve as proof of the "new" work
ethic.

DE VANA GLORIA. Now we come to an entry "De vana gloria," on boasting,
intended to document the virtue of humility, an entry which we could have
easily overlooked in the pursuit of our quest. This section starts with the
story of Henricus of Gouda, the Father Confessor of the Sisters of the
Common Life in Zwolle, who sometimes walked in *clompen* (1.344), the
wooden shoes of the common man – as far as I can see, here referred to for
the first time in Dutch (though identified by the chronicler as a German
word) and implicitly identified as the typical footwear of the lowly. Henricus
displayed the humility of the Brethren by coming into the Grote Kerk in
Zwolle with his wooden shoes, and before ascending the high pulpit to
preach his sermon, he shed his *clompen* at the foot of the stairs (cf. *FH*,
43-44.).

But in the same section we get an intriguing while rewarding report on
the humility of the founder of the movement, Geert Groote himself. Again
introduced with his academic title *magister*, it is soberly pointed out that Geert

---

[35]If this is the same lay brother as described in *FH*, then his interest in learning is not
surprising since he "magschien een meister in den vruen Kunsten was," which means "perhaps
he had earned his MA." *FH*, 183.

is called The Great for no other reason than that was the name of his family. His father, after all (*nam!*), belonged as mayor to the ruling elite of the city of Deventer, and was already known as Werner Groote. But as a young man, magister Geert had, according to reliable testimony, gone to study in Paris and become such an outstanding student that he was second to none in the whole world, be it in the liberal arts, philosophy, ethics, in secular and canon law, as well as in theology: "Nulli secundus esset in orbe" (1.329; cf. *FH* 2). Such high praise of the academic achievements of the founding father would have been completely out of place if the entry had not continued with the conversion of Geert Groote, who "even though he was such a great man of learning" (*talis ac tantus*, 1.330), was henceforth dressed in humble clothing, displaying his state of utter penance and poverty even as an academic in Paris.

Yet, and now the point of the story comes, "there it was that he bought all those books with which he has endowed our library, paying for them so much gold as can be placed in a large wine glass." The interest of the author of the manuscript was obviously directed toward the voluntary character of Groote's poverty, but in the meantime – as it were, unintentionally – he highlighted the fact that Geert, after his conversion, invested a large sum of gold in buying books from which the Brethren profited: "emens ibidem libros de quibus nostra libraria est ditata. . ." (1.333f.; cf. *FH*, 5).[36]

Again, while the author continues to be interested in the record of humility, we are about to learn something else. There was a far more intimate relationship between the Latin school and the Houses of the Brethren than recent scholarship has led us to expect. Post's insistence on the institutional difference between school and Brethren house is amply confirmed, and yet the task of the Brethren and their presence in the schools clearly exceeds the mere supervision of their pupils' school work at night.

The fourth rector of the house in Deventer, Godfried, the third successor of Groote after Radewijns and Amilius, was himself, as is explicitly noted, a former teacher (*fuerat lector in scolis*, 1.310-11). Whenever the relation between School and House is touched upon, the intended – or should one say conscious – thrust is that the Brother concerned is not exempt from the embarrassing dress code, shortened gowns and patched surplices, because of his former status as a teacher (*FH*, 56; cf. 67, 202). But indirectly and by contrast, we learn that to be a teacher at a Latin school was regarded as a high station. Accordingly, it is not surprising that, for instance, the rector

---

[36]The actual course of events is considerably telescoped. Three years after his conversion (1374), Geert trekked for the third time to Paris, where he had received his B.A. (1357) and M.A. (1358), and returned to study law (1362-66). This third time, "perhaps before the end of 1377," he journeyed to Paris to buy the books which, at the end of his life, he donated to the Brethren. See Van Zijl, *Gerard Groote*, 121-22. His splendid original library he had abandoned before his conversion; its "black magic," i.e. astrological books, he publicly burned in the market in Deventer (53). His early delight in learning is, however, as well documented as his later warnings against it.

of the Frater house in Nijmegen, to which in 1475 a school building was added, accepted the obligation to feed *and* teach each year "six poor boys" for a yearly stipend. The contract clearly suggests more than pastoral care.[37]

Another glance at the state of learning gives the entry "De superbia" with the information that magister Geert Groote always insisted on speaking Latin with the Brethren. The fine to be paid for a Dutch slip of the tongue was to kneel down and kiss the earth. This story would of course not have been complete if it did not also refer to the one time that magister Gerardus himself unwittingly made such a slip. As soon as he realized that the Brethren around him had started to giggle – after all, they did not dare to correct him – he immediately threw himself on his knees and kissed the floor (1.380-85).

DE ZELO ANIMARUM. Three recollections under the heading "De zelo animarum" complete our picture. In the case of Geert Groote, the zeal for pastoral care went so far that he did not hesitate to take to sea in order to preach the Gospel. One time, when he wanted to take his message all the way to Holland, the Devil tried to block his route by evoking such a storm over the Zuider Zee (now Ijsselmeer), that Geert was hardly able to save his hand-library which had been carefully packed in a crate to protect the books from water damage (1.522; cf. *FH, 6*).[38]

The most revered Rudolph of Muiden, whom we met before, was known to hate verbosity. He liked to quote from Saint Bernard, "Nuge in secularibus nuge quidem sint, in sacerdotibus autem blasphemie: ferende fortasse nonnunquam, sed nunquam proferende" (*De cons.* 2.22; 1.533-36). Rudolph here continued the medieval crusade *contra nugas*, which in the sixteenth century became the open war against "papist preachers" who replaced the solid food of God's word with idle talk of their own invention.

Petrus Hoorn shared this attitude of extreme reticence, but this did not prevent him from talking at length about holy scripture and the life of the saints, particularly of "our own fathers" (1.547f.). His word had great authority because it was in keeping with the Fathers and with holy scripture: "conforme fuit [consilium suum] sentenciis patrum et sacre scripture testimonio approbatum" (1.562-64); but even more so because his learning was authentic: all of us knew him as a sincere and upright man who gave his counsel in fear of God and in keeping with his conscience ("ex timore Dei et conscientia sua") (1.566-67).

---

[37]The endowment, dated July 1, 1523, describes the duties as "bedwangck ende leringe" – discipline *and* instruction. See Schoengen, *Monasticon Batavum* 2 (as in n. 41 below), 142-43, nr. 14. R. R. Post, *The Modern Devotion*, 609, is inclined to interpret this provision as stipulating "a little supplementary tuition at home from the *repetitor*." His arguments are convincing insofar as even in Nijmegen most of the *scolares* living with the Brethren would have attended the much better endowed city school. But at least one of the Brethren is referred to as "onss schoelmeister" – our school teacher – which goes to show that not only *former* school teachers lived as Brethren.

[38]Cf. van Zijl, *Gerard Groote*, 158-59.

DE PERSEVERANTIA. I conclude with one entry under the heading "De perseverantia," which draws together the several themes touched upon hitherto. The event was written down some eighty years after it occurred in the year 1400. A young man by the name of Stephan[us] came to study in Deventer from the area of Louvain – or rather Leuven, as the Flemish must insist in view of the inroads made by the Francophones. Stephan sought to live the devout life, and was therefore placed by the rector Amilius in a dormitory (*bursa*) with other students under his spiritual direction. However, when Stephan's father came to visit him in Deventer and there discovered that his son had fallen in with the Brethren of the Modern Devotion (*incidere more devotorum*), he became furious.

Unable to change the mind of his son, the father withdrew the money that he had given Stephan for his studies. Absolutely beside himself, the father ran into the main square of Deventer, publicly cursing the Brethren. But God moderated his tongue so [wonderfully] that he started to speak French, even though he knew Dutch very well. Hence, the people did not understand a word of what he was saying. When the son, who had been put into hiding four miles away in Diepenveen – probably in its Sisterhouse – returned to Deventer after his father had left, rector Amilius asked him whether, now that he was penniless, Stephan would be prepared to beg for his food. When the boy said yes, Amilius took pity upon him. He took the boy into the house of the Brethren and made him an associate member of the community (*cum esset ipse Stephanus litterature* [*sic*;1.665]).

Even this last story yields only indirectly the information we seek. The intended point is clearly the perseverance of Stephan and, accordingly, the end of the tale is an expected devout version of living happily ever after: "Stephan, even though young in body, was strong in spirit and zeal for 'our' devout tradition, an example of humility and obedience, exceedingly beloved with almost all the *fratres*." For us, however, the point lies rather in the motivation of the rector. He did not admit Stephan because of his striking humility, but because of his impressive *litterature* – a new, as yet unrecorded word or a fumbled version of *litteratus*. This may mean that Stephan was lettered and well read, or merely that he could read and write. In either case, the story of Stephan supports our findings, and it documents the deep respect and the high ranking of literacy and erudition; for rector Amilius, it made all the difference!

Pietas quaerens intellectum

Such chronicles are storehouses of stories used in the time-honored tradition of *exempla* intended to bridge the gap between the *eruditi* and the *simplices*. They are the perfect literary form for the *medius status* between doctrine and life.

Typical of the *medius status*, the movement existed legally under civic jurisdiction but spiritually in a world between the walls of the monastery and the walls of the city. With its ascetic/practical bent, it had little affinity with the philological expertise of the leading city humanists, but it was explicitly antagonistic to the theology of the monks, with its despised arrogance and verbosity. Hence, the Devotio Moderna stands also intellectually "between the walls," which helps one to understand why the campaign *contra vanam curiositatem*[39] did not yield the anti-intellectualism so long associated with it.

The source we have turned to is not only precious because it allows for glances at daily life in the Brethren community. It also shows us the spectacles with which the earliest Golden Age was viewed one century later, and thus provides us with that ideology of the movement which it wanted to convey, in order to guide the present and gain the next generation. We are only one step removed from the sentiment expressed in a Reformation pamphlet of the year 1523: "When God says 'this is my beloved son, listen to him' (Matt. 17:5), he did not say 'Listen to the monks and the humanists.' No. . . !"[40]

I am inclined to regard the movement of the Brethren and Sisters of the Common Life as a remarkable success. Within the borders of today's Netherlands alone, there were between 1380 and 1480, in the heyday of the movement, two hundred foundations. Of these, thirty-five monasteries and thirty nunneries belonged to the network of the Windesheim Congregation. The extent to which the Devotio Moderna was a women's movement has not been noticed because it was not noted that more than half (105) were communities of the Sisters and only 15 percent (30) establishments of the always much more discussed Brethren of the Common Life.[41] Yet, the mere

---

[39]Cf. my reconstruction of the history of the medieval crusade "against vain curiosity," *Contra vanam curiositatem: Ein Kapitel der Theologie zwischen Seelenwinkel und Weltall* (Zurich: Theologischer Verlag, 1974), esp. 23-32. In a richly documented book-length article, Klaus Schreiner has traced the manifold forms of resistance against the increasing access of the laity to knowledge and erudition in the later Middle Ages. Describing the widely felt sense of *Ungleichheit der Bildung* as *Ausprägung sozialer Ungleichheit*, Schreiner points to the concomitant view of society as divided into two estates: "In 'litterati' und 'illiterati' oder in die 'gelerten' und den 'gemeinen man.'" "Laienbildung als Herausforderung für Kirche und Gesellschaft: Religiöse Vorbehalte und soziale Widerstände gegen die Verbreitung von Wissen im späten Mittelalter und in der Reformation," *Zeitschrift für Historische Forschung* 2 (1984): 257-354; 329.

[40]"Da sagt got nit: höret den munchen ader den humanisten. Nein, höret meinen sun, der ewre sunde am stam des heylgen Creutzs uberwunden hat. . ." *Eynn Dialogus ader gesprech . . .* (Erfurt, 1523), fol. a iii b.

[41]This calculation is based on my computation of the data provided by Michael Schoengen, *Monasticon Batavum* 2: *De Augustijnse orden benevens de Broeders en Zusters van het Gemeene Leven* (Verhandelingen der Nederlandsche Akademie van Wetenschappen, Afd. Letterkunde, N.S. Nr. 45) (Amsterdam, 1941). The numbers indicated do not include the considerable number of houses that joined the Sion congregation, even though often initiated by the *devoti*. For Germany, Gerhard Rehm, *Die Schwestern vom gemeinsamen Leben im nordwestlichen Deutschland:*

tabulation of houses cannot do full justice to the remarkably high percentage of women. For none of the Brethren houses is a head count available which comes close to the Orthenconvent in 's Hertegenbosch where, c. 1450, seven hundred Sisters are reported as each operating her own loom: the first recorded factory in The Netherlands.[42] Though this example highlights the material dimension of voluntary poverty, and generally suggests that *conversio* may not have meant for most *devoti* a radical change in poverty level, there is no reason to doubt the spiritual motivation. The rapid spread of the movement along the fertile crescent to the Rhine and upper Germany can best be explained in terms of its consonance with that pan-European religious revival mobilizing the lay world in the form of fraternities and confraternities, hospital associations, and third orders of well-established monastic organizations.

It has been argued that, around the turn of the century, the *devoti* reached the end of their economic rope since the *scriptorium* could no longer compete with the successful printing presses. But a quick adjustment to the new technique is amply documented by the disproportionately high number of incunabula produced by the Houses.[43] More importantly, the economic motivation for the tradition of transcription has been over-rated. The office

---

Untersuchungen zur Geschichte der Devotio moderna und des weiblichen Religiosentums, Berliner Historische Studien, 11: Ordensstudien, 5. (Berlin, Duncker & Humblot, 1985), has noted sixty-seven Sister houses founded between 1400 and 1500, with an average of fifty members in each. In contrast with my emphasis on the impressive popularity and growth of the Sisters in the Netherlands, Rehm is more restrained in his estimate of their significance as "wenig bedeutsam": "Spektakulär war die Geschichte der Schwestern vom gemeinsamen Leben auch im 15. Jahrhundert nicht" (331). He bases his judgment on the fact that they did not produce "einprägenden Heiligen, Mystikerinnen oder Schriftstellerinnen." I cannot contest this last conclusion, but for two reasons do not regard the argument as convincing. First, for the initiation of the process of canonization, not "die Nachwelt" in general, but a "remembering community" is essential: after the emergence of the Reformation, their "community" faded away. And secondly, the combination of humble social background and non-ostentatious spirituality – programmatically averse to high mysticism – goes far in explaining both the scarcity of exceptional figures and their wide appeal.

[42]At the time of capitulation of Den Bosch to Prince Frederik Hendrik in 1629, the community still comprised 104 Sisters. See Schoengen, *Monasticon*, 97, nr. 23.

[43]See the conclusion of R. H. Rouse, "Backgrounds to Print: Aspects of the Manuscript Book in Northern Europe of the Fifteenth Century," in *Proceedings of the Patristic, Mediaeval and Renaissance Conference* 6 (Villanova, Pa.: Augustinian Historical Institute, Villanova University, 1981), 37-50; 48: "It is due to the Windesheimers and the Brethren, most of all, that the 'new book' achieved a dissemination far beyond the walls of ecclesiastical houses." Rouse not only points to the Fraterhouses as the "market," but also as the "investors" who "hired printers to publish for them" (49). Rouse goes in this judgment far beyond Post, *The Modern Devotion*, 553, who regards the contribution of the *devoti* as "modest," and in comparison with a number of city presses, "quite insignificant." J. P. Gumpert, *Die Utrechter Kartäuser und ihre Bücher im frühen fünfzehnten Jahrhundert* (Leiden: Brill, 1974), 311, however, compares the *devoti* with the Carthusians and comes to the conclusion that ". . . in ihrer Auffassung des praedicare manibus, sind die Devoten wirklich 'modern'" – books are made for the market and not only an ascetic exercise.

of the *scriptor* (*Broeder van den penne*) was, within each house, in such high standing because he or she was in this way involved in the "apostolate of writing" and could thus provide for the daily devotional readings (*rapiaria*) and for the *exempla* used by the speakers at the *collationes* for schoolboys and members alike. Being to such a large extent a community of craftsmen, they could provide for their own needs.

But the lowness of their economic status is reflected in the shocked reaction of the Flemish father of Stephan, who was driven to French curses when he learned with what kind of people his son had come to associate. However, the income of the *devoti* was not primarily based on the writing and selling of books, but on their own artifacts and, when necessary, on the mendicant life. At times the Brethren went door to door to beg for bread. One of them, John Kessel, liked to shout, "Give a poor pilgrim something for his trek to Jerusalem." Afraid of being misunderstood by his readers, the chronicler was quick to add that Kessel meant his pilgrimage to the eternal Jerusalem (1.708-10; cf. *FH*, 47). Indeed, the *devoti* were not interested in any other career than their progress *in via* to the eternal Jerusalem – an arduous path on which, to use the simile of Saint Augustine, a load of knowledge is only a burden, slowing down the pilgrim.

Yet, since about the middle of the fifteenth century a new dimension emerged when the young generation started to give account of the history of its own movement and to emphasize along with scripture and the Fathers that glorious part of the tradition of their own fathers which was available to them in the *Gesta* of the founding fathers. The *rapiaria* are no longer a loose collection of biblical sayings, and the chronicles are no longer just a list of entries enumerating the offices held, with the death dates for the Brethren and Sisters. They start to become that kind of historical source which in all cultures provides for the matrix of new learning.

Through the establishment of the canons regular in Windesheim (1387) – the third, in some ways perhaps even most important branch[44] – the movement provided the impetus for reform of long-established monastic orders, by supporting what was called at that time "the Observance."[45] In all the Observant wings of the orders, which developed after the Council of Constance (1414-18), the new emphasis on the original *regula* went hand

---

[44]Thus argued by C. van der Wansem, *Het ontstaan en de geschiedenis der Broederschap van het Gemene Leven tot 1400* (Leuven: Universiteitsbibliotheek, 1958), 96-97.

[45]The impact of the Windesheim Congregation went well beyond the Observants. See e.g. Kaspar Elm, *Beiträge zur Geschichte der Wilhelmitenordens* (Cologne: Böhlau, 1962), 144-45. At times, the impact was mutual, as in the case of Henri Herp who joined, in 1450, the Observant Franciscans after having served as rector of the Brethren house in Delft. His sermons do not mark him as a deviant. See the critical edition of Georgette Epiney-Burgard, ed., *Henri Herp: De Processu humani profectus: Sermones de diversis materiis vitae contemplativae* (Wiesbaden: F. Steiner, 1982). For the cooperation and exchange between the Windesheim Congregation and the Benedictine Bursfeld Congregation, see Nicolaus C. Heutger, *Bursfelde und seine Reformklöster in Niedersachsen* (Hildesheim: A. Lax, 1969), 25ff.

in hand with a renewed interest in the origins of the order and its original intentions. The concomitant study of the scriptures and of the Fathers, with all the available "modern" tools, did not usually lead to a return to scholasticism as we find it in the coalition of the *Devotio Moderna* and the *Via Moderna* in Tübingen. More often, it led to some form of what can best be called monastic humanism.[46] It developed a new sensitivity to erudition as the knowledge of the sources of wisdom (*sapientia*), if not of secular inquiry (*scientia*).[47]

One story – inconceivable a hundred years before – may serve at the same time as illustration and summary. It is tucked away in an overlooked entry in the Frensweger manuscript, a chronicle which breaks off at the death of Reyner of Texel († 1483), the third rector of Albergen (near Ootmarsum, Twente). Like most of the Brethren, Reyner is presented as originally a simple man; he was unschooled before his conversion. But after he came to the Brethren, he started to study all the books in the library so assiduously "that he became a formidable authority in all the arts and sciences."[48] This story is the exact inversion of the earliest legend about the Founding Father, Geert Groote, who was as learned before conversion as the devout Reyner afterwards.

We stumble here over a law perhaps characteristic of the piety of all "book" religions. The history of the Modern Devotion, together with its indirect continuation in the Observant movement, reflects that same curve which one can observe in the development of medieval monasticism after the days of Saint Bernard († 1153). Bernard's vociferous campaign *contra nugas* in the twelfth century did not prevent the next generation of disciples from becoming fully involved in the scientific investigation of nature; and the warning of Saint Francis († 1226), *scientia inflat*, in the thirteenth century, did not prevent the next generation of Franciscan friars from becoming eminent university professors.

[46]Cf. Noel L. Brann, *The Abbott Trithemius (1462-1516): The Renaissance of Monastic Humanism*, SHCTh 24 (Leiden: Brill, 1981), esp. 218-21.

[47]William Bouwsma, "The Renaissance and the Broadening of Communication," in *Propaganda and Communication in World History*, ed. Harold D. Lasswell (Honolulu: University of Hawaii Press, 1980), 2:3-40; 22, goes even a step further in closing the gap: "But the differences even between earlier Italy and the rest of Europe were not absolute. The movement known as the *Devotio Moderna*, which spread from the Low Countries into much of northern Europe in the fifteenth century, suggests that everywhere townsmen were discontent with the specialized and inaccessible subtleties of scholastic discourse and craved a spiritual and moral guidance that spoke directly to their condition in a language they could understand; this need found prominent expression in the *Imitation of Christ* by Thomas à Kempis. The schoolmasters of this movement, the Brethren of the Common Life, showed an interest in classical texts that paralleled that of the humanists in Italy."

[48]"Hie was weynich gheleert doe hie yn der scholen was ende ter bekieringe quam, meer hie hadde wonderlick groet natuerlick verstant, ende toe hie toe Alberghen totter armer vergadderinghe ghecomen was soe was hie soe seer vlitich te lesen ende doer te siene alle boeke ende schriften, dat hie soe wijs ende wittich wart dat hie by nae van allen scriften, wijshheiten ende konsten, zeer vele wiste." *FH*, 259.

Similarly, the Modern Devotion started out in the fourteenth century by taking over the battle cry of Saint Bernard and Saint Francis against secular scholarship as a real threat to true devotion. But once again, the defense of true devotion led to such an involvement in learning that the very effort to ward off its concomitant dangers required an intellectual concentration which became the bedrock of a new erudition. It may not give way to our modern notion of secular scholarship, but it most certainly fostered a "pietas quaerens intellectum."

We started our quest for the popular impact of learned culture with the assumption of a social hierarchy in which learning was the privilege of the elite, reaching the lower echelons of society only at the time of Renaissance and Reformation. The evidence presented rather points to a dialectical movement in which, by reaction to high culture and its claims to scholarship, the unschooled common man – in this case primarily the artisan and craftsman – in his search for holiness first rejected the rational rule of the "establishment" and then in response developed an impatient thirst for information which, by the beginning of the sixteenth century, came to yield its own kind of broad-based intellectual sense and sensibility.

The common man was by no means just a plebeian reduced to abject poverty – even though Groote saw this dimension quite clearly.[49] When our sources refer to the common man – or as the Frenswegen manuscript put it in Dutch, the *ghemeyne volck* (FH,8) – that kind of simple, underprivileged, and uninformed folk is intended from which the *devoti* recruited, and with which they associated themselves. Along the road of voluntary poverty, a new self-esteem grew which did not lay claim to academic titles, but succeeded in forming its own "intelligentsia." Reformation propaganda found a ready and alert audience, as is succinctly formulated in one of the most impressive Reformation pamphlets: "Don't believe them when they say, 'ja, die bawren verstehen die sach nicht.'"[50]

---

[49]Against the "much heralded" missions of the mendicants to the pagan world outside of "Christian" Europe, Geert Groote, *Epistolae,* pitched his "much more needed" mission to the poor in Christian territories: ". . . unde michi visum est simplices pauperes et abiectos et ignaros magno fervore et labore amplecti debere, qui et quanto nudiores ab altis fastigiis tanto verbi Dei receptibiliores sunt. . . ." See van Zijl, *Gerard Groote.* As later with Thomas Müntzer († 1525), poverty in body and poverty in spirit are not (yet) split up. Cf. Schreiner, "Laienbildung als Herausforderung für Kirche und Gesellschaft," 320.

[50]*Eynn Dialogus ader gesprech.* . . (Erfurt, 1523), fol. a ii b.

Ein neuwer Spruch/ wie die Geystlichheit vnd etlich Handtwercker vber den Luther clagen.

Der geitzig clagt auß falschem mût/
Seit jm abget an Eer vnd Gût.
Er zürnet/ Dobet/ vnde Wüt/
In dürstet nach des grechten plût.

Die warheit ist Got vnd sein wort/
Das pleibt ewiglich vnzerstort.
Wie jer die Gotloß auch rumort/
Gott bschützt sein diener hie vnd dort.

Der Grecht sagt die Gotlich warheit/
Wie hart man jn veruolgt/verleit.
hofft er in Gott doch alle zeit/
Pleibt bstendig in der grechtigkeit.

Die clag der Gotlosen.

Hör vnser clag du strenger Richter/
Vnd sey vnser zwitrachts ein schlichter.
Eb wir die hend selb legen an/
Martin Luther den schedlich man/
Der hatt geschrifen vnd gelert/
Vnd schir das gätz Teütsch land verkert.
Mit schmehen/lestern/nach vnd weit/
Die Erwirdig Gaistlichhait.
Von jren Pfründen/ Rent vnd zinst/
Vnd verwürfft auch jren Gotdinst.
Der Vätter gepot/ vnd auffsatz/
haist er vnns/ vnd menschen gschwetz/
helt nichts von Ziplaß vnd Fegfewr/
Die Meß kum auch kain Sel zu stewr.
All Kirchen Perw/ Zir/ vnd gschmuck/
Veracht er gar/ es ist nie cluck.
Des clagen die Prelaten set/
Pfaffen/Münch/ Stationier.
Glockengiesser vnd Organisten/
Goltschlager vnd Illuministen/
Nadtmaler/ Goltschmit vn bildschnitzer/
Ratschmit/ Glaßmaler/ seyden sitzer.
Stainmetzen/Zimerleüt Schriner/
Paternoster/ Kertzen macher.
Die Permenter/ Singer vnd Schreyber/
Fischer/ zopffman vnd pfaffen Weyber/
Den allen ist Luther ein gschwer/
Von dir wir tun Vrtail begern.
Sunst werde wir weiter Appellieren/
Vnd dem Luther die Piend recht schirn/
Müß Pümen/ oder Reuocirn.

Antwort .D. Martini.

Hebreum.1.
O da allermer aller hertzen/
Hör mein antwort des ist kein schertzen.
Die schreyen fast ich thûn mich stewn/
Vnd wöllen doch mit Disputirn.
Sonder mich mit worten schmucken/
In thut we das ich thu auff deckn.
Ir grossen geytz vnd Simoney/
Ir falsch Gotdinst vnd Gleissnerey.
Ir Bannen/ Auffsatz vnd gepot/
Vor aller welt zu schand vnd spott.
Mit deinem wort/ das ich denn ler/
Nan jn abgeet an gut vnd Eer.
So fanden sy dein wort nit leiden/
Dann mich schelten/hassen vnd neiden/
Wenn ich hett gschwifen vnd gelert/
Das sich jr Reich vnd heer gemert.
So wer kein Besser auff gestandn/
In langer zeit in Teutschen Landn.
Dis ist auch die r isach ich sag/
Das gegen mir auch stent in clag.
Der Hantwerck leit ein grosse zal/
Den auch abget in disem val.
Seyt diß Apgötterey entnimpt/
Also seynd vber mich ergrimt.

3.Regū.18.
Actuū.19.
Von erst des Baals Tempel knecht/
Den jr jarmarck thut nimmer recht.
Vnd Demetrius der werckman/
Dem sein handtwerck zu ruck wil gan.
Her durch dein wort das ich thu schreibn/
Ir disen soll mich nit abtreibn/
Bey deinem vrteil will ich pleibn.

hans Sachs Schuster.

Das Vrteil Christi.

Joānis.5.
Das mein gericht das ist gerecht/
Nu merck vermaints gaistliche geslecht.
Was ich euch selb bevolhen han/
Das jr in die gantz welt solt gan.

Mar. vitio.
Predigen aller Creatur/
Das Euangeli rain vnd pur.
Dasselbig hant jr gar verachte/
Vnd vil newer Gotdinst auff pracht.

Mathei.15.
Der ich doch kein geheissen hab/
Vnd verkaufft sie vns gelt vnd gab.

Math.23.
Den witwen jr die hewser fressen/
Vnd verspert auch das Himelreich/
Ir seyt den Doten grebern gleich.
Diß schlacht zu dot auch mein propheten/
Der gleich die Pharisser thetten/
Also verwolgt jr die warhait/

Luce.13.
Die euch teglichen wirt geseit.
Vnd so jr euch nit pessern wort/
Ir virkumen/Darumb so kart.
Von euwerm falschen widerstreit/
Dergleichen jr handtwerck leyt.
Die jr mein wort veracht mit drug/
Von wegen ewoß aygen nug.

Mathei.6.
Vnd hört doch in den worten mein/
Das jr nit sole sorgfeldig sein.
Vmb zeitlich güt/ gleich den Haydn/
Söder sucht das Reich gots mit freudn/
Das zeitlich wirt euch wol zufalln/
Sunst wert jr in der hellen qualln/
Das ist mein vrteil zu euch alln.

Luther and the Artisans, c. 1525 Nuremberg.
Verses by Hans Sachs

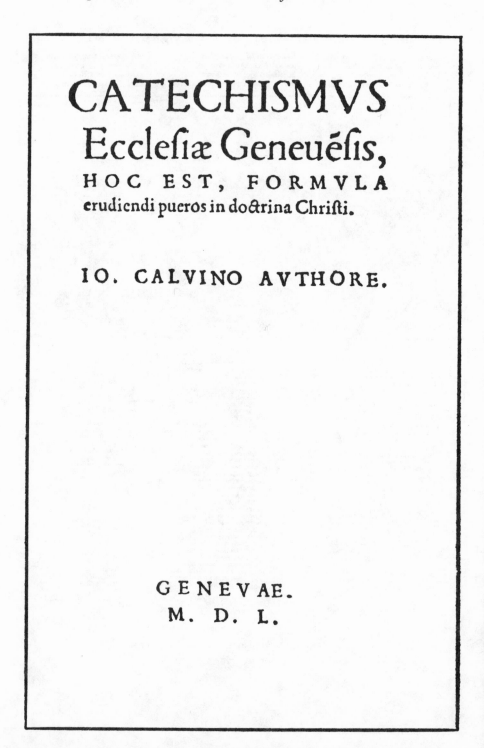

CATECHISMVS
Ecclefiæ Geneuéfis,
HOC EST, FORMVLA
erudiendi pueros in doctrina Chrifti.

IO. CALVINO AVTHORE.

GENEVAE.
M. D. L.

The Peculiarity of the Reformation in Geneva

William J. Bouwsma

RECENT STUDY of the adherence of towns to what was eventually to be called Protestantism has been fairly successful in identifying common patterns by which this was accomplished.[1] But when a Whiggish assumption that the conquest of Protestantism was everywhere popular leads to over-generalization, difficulties arise. We may then forget, to paraphrase a great observer of the sixteenth-century scene, that although no towns were born Protestant and some towns achieved Protestantism, others had Protestantism thrust upon them. Geneva belonged to this last group, compelled to turn Protestant by political circumstances rather than by any significant wave of evangelical fervor. In this respect Geneva differed markedly from neighboring towns, notably from the more typical Basel and Strasbourg.

Our association of these three communities has been natural, not only because of their neighborhood but also because all three harbored John Calvin during significant moments of his life. When he left France in 1535, he followed his friend Nicolas Cop to Basel, attracted there, like Erasmus, by its scholarly atmosphere, the presence of other learned Frenchmen, and the prospect of a peaceful life of study.[2] In Basel he perfected his Greek and Hebrew, composed his lyrical prefaces to the French Bible of his cousin Olivétan, and wrote and published the first version of the *Institutes*.[3] He had been heading for Strasbourg when Farel waylaid him in Geneva; and he spent three years there after his expulsion from Geneva in 1538, in what, in spite of his ignorance of German, was perhaps the happiest interval in an otherwise harried existence.[4] He might well have remained in Strasbourg for the rest of his life but for an unexpected shift in the political climate in

---

[1]The increasing refinement of this enterprise can be traced through Bernd Moeller, *Reichsstadt und Reformation* (Gutersloh: Gerd Mohn, 1962); Steven E. Ozment, *The Reformation in the Cities: The Appeal of Protestantism to Sixteenth-Century Germany and Switzerland* (New Haven: Yale University Press, 1975); Thomas A. Brady, Jr., *Ruling Class, Regime and Reformation at Strasbourg* (Leiden: Brill, 1978), and *Turning Swiss: Cities and Empire, 1450-1550* (New York: Cambridge University Press, 1985).

[2]Cf. Eugenie Droz, "Jean Calvin à Bâle (décembre 1534 à fin mars 1536)," *Chemins de l'hérésie: Textes et documents*, 4 vols. (Geneva: Slatkine, 1970-76), 1:89-129. For the atmosphere of Basel and its attraction for learned Frenchmen generally, see Peter G. Bietenholz, *Basle and France in the Sixteenth Century: The Basle Humanists and Printers in Their Contacts with Francophone Culture* (Geneva: Droz, 1971).

[3]Alexander Ganoczy, *Le jeune Calvin: Genèse et évolution de sa vocation réformatrice* (Wiesbaden: Steiner, 1966), 84-97, gives unusual attention to Calvin's Basel period. Now also in English: *The Young Calvin*, trans. David Foxgrover and Wade Provo (Philadelphia: Westminster Press, 1987).

[4]On this point I agree with Benoît Girardin, *Rhétorique et théologie: Calvin, le Commentaire de l'Epitre aux Romains* (Paris: Beauchesne, 1979), 102-3.

Geneva and the insistence of his mentor, Martin Bucer, that he return. In Geneva Calvin complained of how much he had to do; in Strasbourg his accounts of busy days seem more like boasting.[5] But it may also be assumed that he drew conclusions, from the establishment of the Reformation in Basel and Strasbourg, applicable to the reform of Geneva.

The peculiarity of the Genevan Reformation is most obvious in its origin and results.[6] Geneva was neither a German, a free, nor an imperial city; and its adherence to Protestantism did not occur until 1536, whereas most other towns sided with the Reformers after the Peasants' War. Finally, what was accomplished in Geneva was done without the support of native clergy; indeed, no Genevan served as a pastor in the city between 1536 and the end of the century.[7] The outcome of the Reformation in Geneva was even more extraordinary. In every other Protestant city, as far as I know, the Reformation culminated in what Heiko Oberman has described as "the priesthood of all qualified councilmen";[8] only in Geneva did the clergy – the fact that they were, without exception, aliens is thus doubly significant – succeed in establishing, through the power of excommunication, effective control over an urban church. And this meant that only in Geneva was an urban church able to rise above the local preoccupations that were dominant elsewhere and to set in motion a singularly dynamic international movement. The explanation for these anomalies requires us to consider the very different outcomes in Basel and Strasbourg.

Basel and Strasbourg were, of course, not alike in every respect. For one thing, Basel, with a population of about ten thousand, was less than half as large as Strasbourg. But both were free imperial cities and important commercial centers in which the guild revolts of the later Middle Ages had

[5]Cf. his letter to Farel, April 20, 1539: "I do not remember throughout this whole year a single day which was more completely engaged with various occupations. For when the present messenger wished to carry along with him the beginning of my book [probably the second edition of the *Institutes*], there were about twenty leaves which I needed to revise. In addition there was the public lecture, and I had also to preach; four letters were also to be written, some disputes to settle, and more than ten interruptions to reply to in the meantime." *CO*, 10:337. (Calvin's letters are in *Johannis Calvini Opera quae supersunt omnia*, 59 vols., ed. Guilielmus Baum, et al. [Brunswick, 1863-1900], cited here as *CO*).

[6]The fullest account of its origins is Henri Naef, *Les origines de la Réforme à Genève* (Geneva: Droz, 1968). E. William Monter, *Calvin's Geneva* (New York: Wiley, 1967) provides an admirably balanced account. Robert M. Kingdon, *Geneva and the Coming of the Wars of Religion in France, 1555-1563* (Geneva: Droz, 1956), and Carlos M.N. Eire, *War Against the Idols: The Reformation of Worship from Erasmus to Calvin* (New York: Cambridge University Press, 1986) are also useful for particular aspects of the Genevan Reformation.

[7]Gillian Lewis notes this in "Calvinism in the Time of Calvin and Beza, 1541-1608," *International Calvinism, 1541-1715*, ed. Menna Prestwich (New York: Oxford University Press, 1985), 47.

[8]"Die Reformation als theologische Revolution," *Zwingli und Europa: Referate und Protokoll des Internationalen Kongresses aus Anlass des 500. Geburtstages von Huldrych Zwingli vom 26 bis 30 März 1984*, ed. Peter Blickle, Andreas Lindt, and Alfred Schindler (Zurich: Vandenhoeck & Ruprecht, 1985), 19.

succeeded in establishing communal governments. These were generally dominated by patrician elites, although the artisan guilds of Basel seem to have had a larger voice in government than was the case in Strasbourg.[9]

Neither town, on the eve of the Reformation, seemed ripe for religious revolution, although the moralizing sermons of Johann Geiler and the Franciscan Thomas Murner's attacks on clerical vices may have promoted a sharper anticlericalism in and around Strasbourg than prevailed elsewhere.[10] The ruling groups in both towns were closely allied with the old ecclesiastical order, like ruling groups elsewhere, partly because it left the practical administration of the church largely to the municipal authorities, but also, as Brady has suggested, because of the deep familial and fiscal connections between the church and other ruling groups.[11]

They were also alike – and in this respect not altogether typical of the cities that turned to Protestantism – in that both, well before the Reformation, were centers of the printing industry. By the beginning of the sixteenth century, more than seventy printers were working in Basel, including such great figures as Amerbach and Froben. The printers of Basel supplied an international market and were especially well regarded in France.[12] As we know from Miriam Chrisman, Strasbourg's presses also produced books of every kind, literary, scientific, and religious, in Latin and the vernacular, especially in the first two decades of the sixteenth century.[13]

These books, to be sure, especially those representing learned culture, were not, on the whole, for local consumption; but their publication brought to Basel and Strasbourg learned men, especially humanists qualified for such essential tasks as editing and proofreading. In Basel Erasmus was only the most distinguished of these; he liked Basel because it brought together men he found congenial. As he wrote in 1516 of this group,

> They all know Latin, they all know Greek, most of them Hebrew too; one is an expert historian, another an experienced theologian; one is skilled in mathematics, one a keen antiquary, another a jurist. . . . I certainly have never before had the luck to live in such

[9]Brady, *Strasbourg*, 53-196; Lorna Jane Abray, *The People's Reformation: Magistrates, Clergy, and Commons in Strasbourg, 1500-1598* (Ithaca: Cornell University Press, 1985), 50-58; Hans Guggisberg, *Basel in the Sixteenth Century* (St. Louis: Center for Reformation Research, 1982), 3-27.

[10]Abray, *People's Reformation*, 25-26; Brady, *Strasbourg*, 215-16.

[11]Brady, *Strasbourg*, 217-19; Miriam U. Chrisman, *Strasbourg and the Reform* (New Haven: Yale University Press, 1967), 35-55. For the conservative reform proposals advanced in Strasbourg on the eve of the Reformation, see also Abray, *People's Reformation*, 27-29. On the conservatism of the ruling group in Basel, cf. Ozment, *Reformation in the Cities*, 11.

[12]Bietenholz, *Basle and France*, 20-53; Guggisberg, *Basel*, 9-11.

[13]Miriam Usher Chrisman, *Lay Culture, Learned Culture: Books and Social Change in Strasbourg, 1480-1599* (New Haven: Yale University Press, 1982).

gifted company. And to say nothing of that, how open-hearted they
are, how gay, how well they get on together! You would say they
had only one soul.[14]

This was surely rhetorical exaggeration, and it is doubtless true that such
scholarly personages constituted an isolated group of little interest to the
general population of Basel; they were not called on, as in some cities, even
to serve in the local chancery, much less to celebrate the achievements of
the community.[15] It is difficult, nevertheless, to believe that the harmonizing
bent of these philological humanists, with their Erasmian interest in both
Greek philosophy and Scripture, was irrelevant to the relatively tolerant and
conciliatory atmosphere that Basel retained throughout much of the century.
The local clergy participated significantly in this learned culture.

The situation was not much different in Strasbourg where, although
Sebastian Brant served as City Advocate and City Secretary, there were few
educated men in the regime.[16] But, like Basel, Strasbourg was a center of
humanist activity. The humanists of Strasbourg during the earlier years of
the century, like Brant and Wimpheling, were mostly clergy who were
chiefly interested in the classics as the basis of a new educational program,
but on the eve of the Reformation this interest was shifting toward biblical
studies under the influence of Erasmus and the expanding needs of the
printing industry.[17]

With the onset of agitation for the Reformation, however, the
significance of this learned culture became apparent. In Basel, after 1520,
local clergy began to preach evangelical sermons in the cathedral as well as
in several churches; and a movement to which artisan guilds provided some
popular support eventually found a spiritual leader in Oecolampadius, a
humanist whose mother was from Basel, who had worked for Froben and
assisted Erasmus with his New Testament, and who, with Konrad Pellikan,
a man much like himself, was appointed Professor of Theology by the town
council in 1523. By 1525 the Mass had been abolished in most of Basel's
churches. The town council, which admired Erasmus, had sought to avoid
taking sides for as long as possible. It had been put off by the radicalism of
Guillaume Farel, who, after his rejection by the Meaux circle in 1523, had
proceeded to Basel. He was there given an initial hearing, but he alarmed
even those who, like Oecolampadius, were most sympathetic to the Reform;
partly because of the violence of his attacks on Erasmus, he was expelled

[14]Letter to Johannes Sapidus, February 1516, quoted by Guggisberg, *Basel*, 14.

[15]Cf. Guggisberg, *Basel*, 16-17.

[16]Brady, *Strasbourg*, 189-91.

[17]Abray, *People's Reformation*, 30-31; Chrisman, *Lay Culture, Learned Culture*, 44-47, 92-102;
for Wimpheling's conservatism, see Lewis W. Spitz, *The Religious Renaissance of the German
Humanists* (Cambridge, Mass.: Harvard University Press, 1963), 41, 49.

from Basel the next year.[18] But rioting and iconoclasm on the part of guildsmen, whose demands for religious change were accompanied by pressure for a more democratic government, finally compelled Basel's city fathers, in 1529, to break definitively with the old church and promise a more broadly based polity. This promise was, however, not kept; and by 1530 the power of the old oligarchy was fully restored. Indeed, it had been significantly enlarged to include absolute control over a fully municipal church.[19]

The pattern of Reformation in Strasbourg was much the same, at once in origin, timing, development, and outcome. Members of the local clerical establishment, mostly biblical humanists and followers of Erasmus, began to preach against the ways of the old church in 1521 – though attacking its institutional structures rather than its doctrines. Notable among these priests were Mathias Zell, a preacher in the cathedral whose respectability is suggested by his eventual marriage into a patrician family, and Wolfgang Capito, also a cathedral preacher as well as provost of Saint Thomas.[20] Martin Bucer, another Alsatian though not a Strasbourgeois, arrived in 1523. These men won significant support, and eventually the radicalism and the actual disorders stimulated by the Peasants' War persuaded a divided town council that the only alternative to a complete breakdown of social order was abolition of the Mass. It was immediately eliminated in all but four churches – exceptions which suggest the ambivalence of the regime – but the ban became absolute in 1529. All decisions about such matters, as in Basel, remained with the magistrates. By 1533 they were also making decisions about doctrine; they appointed pastors; and lay courts assumed jurisdiction over offenses previously adjudicated by church courts. Clerical excommunication in Strasbourg, as Abray puts it, "was reduced to a half measure, purged of its power to inflict social ostracism." The acquisition of citizenship by the ministers had as its chief result that they became civic employees, their opinions, their sermons, and their behavior closely monitored.[21]

The aftermath of the Reformation in these two towns was also similar: both had ruling councils controlled by patriciates primarily motivated – as they had been in opting for Protestantism – by a concern for public order, on which their own positions depended. Their towns had been by no means religiously homogeneous; the councils continued to avoid for as long as

[18]Bietenholz, *Basle and France*, 91-93.

[19]On the Reformation in Basel, see Guggisberg, *Basel*, 21-34, and Eire, *War Against the Idols*, 114-19.

[20]On Capito, see James Kittelson, *Wolfgang Capito: From Humanist to Reformer* (Leiden: Brill, 1975).

[21]Abray, *People's Reformation*, 45-49. The best narrative account of the Reformation in Strasbourg remains that of Chrisman, *Strasbourg and the Reform,* but this summary also draws on Abray, Brady, and Kittelson.

possible unequivocal decisions that might provoke domestic religious crises. The result was a kind of practical Erasmian pluralism and toleration in which regimes balanced or oscillated between Zwinglianism and Lutheranism. Meanwhile they ignored nonconformity, whether sectarian or Catholic, unless it insisted on calling attention to itself. Basel gave Erasmus an enthusiastic welcome on his return in 1535; and Myconius, the successor to Oecolampadius as leader of the church in Basel, gave his funeral sermon. The printers of Basel continued to publish Erasmus's works as well as those of other Catholics, and Castellio found employment there after his departure from Geneva. When Montaigne passed through Basel in the fall of 1580, he noted in his journal that the many learned men he met there "were not in agreement over their religion, some calling themselves Zwinglians, others Calvinists, others Martinists"; indeed he was informed that "many still fostered the Roman religion in their heart." He also observed that the images on the exteriors of the churches of Basel, the crosses on their belfries, stained glass windows, tombs, organs, and bells remained intact.[22] Basel nevertheless managed to remain on reasonably good terms with Geneva, in spite of Calvin's attacks on its policies. It continued, therefore, to be a center for a cosmopolitan learned culture. Its interest had been served by a refusal to make the hard, principled choices that a more militant Protestantism demanded elsewhere; its very cosmopolitanism thus served local needs. A less genial expression of its localism was a conspicuous lack of hospitality to religious refugees.[23]

Strasbourg exhibited similar tendencies. Till the end of the century, its citizens remained divided between Swiss and Saxon doctrine; and, lacking a public norm of belief until the latter half of the century, a wide range of religious positions persisted in the ruling group. Church attendance continued to be voluntary.[24] Meanwhile the schools of Strasbourg remained under lay control; and the famous *gymnasium* of Jean Sturm institutionalized the Latin culture of pre-Reformation humanism, with its concern to harmonize classical and Christian literature.[25]

*   *   *

A sharp contrast with Geneva is implicit in this account of the Reformation in Basel and Strasbourg, and in the rest of this article I should like to account for this contrast by describing the rather different conditions of the Reformation in Geneva. The essential point lies, I think in the relative political and cultural backwardness of Geneva; socially, except that it was

---

[22]In the translation of Donald Frame, *The Complete Works of Montaigne* (Stanford: Stanford University Press, 1948), 878-79.

[23]Guggisberg, *Basel,* 38-40, 45-46; Bietenholz, *Basle and France,* 15, 37, 95-97, 122-36.

[24]Abray, *People's Reformation,* 30-31, 40-41; Brady, *Strasbourg,* 233, 246-49.

[25]Chrisman, *Lay Culture, Learned Culture,* 192-201.

less prosperous, Geneva did not seem to differ much from Basel and Strasbourg.[26]

Geneva, the largest community in the lands claimed by the Dukes of Savoy, was, before the Reformation, about the same size as Basel.[27] Whereas most towns ruled by bishops had liberated themselves from episcopal control a century or two earlier, the temporal sovereignty of the bishop of Geneva had remained largely intact; it had only been supplemented, not replaced, by a charter of 1387 that had established a series of councils composed of Genevan citizens; but these had only limited autonomy. The authority of the bishop was threatened less by the citizens of Geneva than by the house of Savoy, which for some decades before the Reformation had controlled the bishopric and, through it, the city.

The political backwardness of Geneva was paralleled by its cultural backwardness. The town had an elementary school before the Reformation, but this offered little more than the rudiments of Latin grammar, and its rector – necessarily an outsider since no Genevan was qualified for the position – had a hard time collecting his fees from the parents of his pupils.[28] Nor was Geneva a printing center; it had, before the arrival of Calvin, a handful of presses, but these printed only religious texts, schoolbooks, and chivalric romances for local consumption, not scholarly books.[29] The only significant thinker who resided in Geneva even briefly before its turn to Protestantism was Cornelius Agrippa, who arrived in 1521, found there a few friends, chiefly among the clergy, and left in 1523, though he had been made a citizen, having failed to gain the patronage of the Duke of Savoy.[30]

This cultural backwardness doubtless helps to explain the slowness with which Geneva responded to new religious possibilities. In Basel and Strasbourg humanists had been among the earliest adherents of the Reform, and local clergy nourished by Erasmianism had prepared the way for the Reformation by preaching evangelical doctrine to a receptive laity. In Geneva the clergy had displayed little interest in the new ideas.[31]

[26]Cf. the characterization of Geneva in Harro M. Höpfl, *The Christian Polity of John Calvin* (New York: Cambridge University Press, 1982), 129.

[27]Naef, *Réforme à Genève*, 1:22-30; Monter, *Geneva*, 2-4.

[28]Naef, *Réforme à Genève*, 1:294-95.

[29]Naef, *Réforme à Genève*, 1:300-2; Robert M. Kingdon, "The Business Activities of Printers Henri and François Estienne," *Aspects de la propagande religieuse* (Geneva: Droz, 1957), 259-73, provides some explanation for Geneva's backwardness in this respect.

[30]Charles G. Nauert, Jr., *Agrippa and the Crisis of Renaissance Thought* (Urbana: University of Illinois Press, 1965), 73-79.

[31]Cf. Eire, *War Against the Idols*, 125-30. Naef, *Réforme à Genève*, 1:462-68, 2:86-91, notes some early Genevan sympathy with the Reformation; but cf. 1:135-55, 171-79, 192-208, for the strength of traditional piety in Geneva.

Instead of engaging in religious reformation, the Genevans, between 1526 and 1536, were carrying out a political revolution that had, immediately, no religious dimension. During the years when other cities were perplexed by the revolution of the common man, Genevans were threatened by the Duke of Savoy, who sought to withdraw their chartered liberties and to transfer the selection of the town syndics, previously elected by an assembly of citizens, to the bishop, whom he controlled. The townsmen responded to this by forming an alliance, in 1526, with Bern, which became officially Protestant two years later. Meanwhile the bishop of Geneva withdrew from the town, well over a century later than this had occurred in neighboring episcopal towns, and Savoy's efforts to recover control subjected Geneva to what was virtually a state of siege lasting for a decade. The religious issue emerged in this tangled situation chiefly because of pressure from Bern, which sought the extension of the Reformation to Geneva. Religious change was also favored by the fact that continued adherence to the old faith would have insured the return of Geneva's prince-bishop and the restoration of control by Savoy.[32]

The clergy in Geneva had displayed little interest in religious change; the few partisans of the Reformation in the town were laymen. Protestant doctrines reached Geneva, therefore, not through local preachers already respected and popular; they were chiefly introduced by outsiders dispatched from Bern. First to arrive was Guillaume Farel, who, after his expulsion from Basel, had preached in various cities in French-speaking Switzerland under the sponsorship of Bern. He came to Geneva in 1532; but, his message unacceptable even at this relatively late date to the conservative Genevans, he was promptly ejected. It has been generally overlooked that his expulsion from Geneva in 1538, along with Calvin, was not his first such experience. Meanwhile another French Reformer, Antoine Froment, had come into the town and also been expelled. Bern then sent the milder Pierre Viret, a French-speaking Swiss, though not a Genevan, who had been educated in Paris. The town council did what it could to resist these pressures from Bern by inviting a noted Dominican, Georges Furbity, as Advent preacher at the end of 1533; but Bern objected so strongly to his sermons that the council was forced to agree to a public disputation early in 1534, and then to another in June of the following year. Meanwhile the ducal forces had made another major attack on the town, and by the fall of 1535 Geneva was threatened by famine.

It was under these difficult circumstances, so different from what occurred in most Protestant towns, that there was now repeated in Geneva much the same sequence of events that had brought the Reformation to a

---

[32]Höpfl, *Christian Polity of Calvin,* 129-33, provides a particularly perceptive summary of this situation. For details see Naef, *Réforme à Genève,* 1:124-30, 1:406-41. On the power of Bern in this period see Brady, *Turning Swiss,* 13.

climax elsewhere. The council was now helpless to resist Farel's return, and his preaching now stimulated the familiar iconoclastic riots; and the Mass, with the enemy at the gates and disorder within, was finally suppressed by the still dubious and reluctant magistrates. The impulse behind this action is suggested by the arrival, a few weeks later, of a Bernese army and the swift defeat of the troops of Savoy. A treaty the following summer recognized the independence of Geneva from Savoy; she became, instead, a vassal of Bern.[33] In addition – and here too the Genevan case contrasts sharply with the situation elsewhere – the handful of Protestant pastors from outside assumed control over the Geneva church. With the abolition of the Mass, almost all the Catholic clergy who had remained, including most parish priests, left the city; and the few who stayed were relieved of clerical duties on the ground that none was sufficiently "educated" for a proper ministry: presumably, that is, because none was sufficiently Protestant. The contrast here with Basel and Strasbourg is particularly striking.[34]

Adherence to the Reformation, therefore, made Geneva into a kind of religious vacuum which an alien clergy rushed to fill. This helps to explain the passionate urgency with which Farel summoned the young and reluctant Calvin to come to his assistance. It also helps to explain the peculiar historical importance of Geneva. The leaders of the church in Geneva would remain, during the whole of the sixteenth century, men without local connections or local loyalties, and accordingly with far larger religious horizons than Protestant clergy elsewhere.[35] These ministers also welcomed, in spite of local objections, a flood of immigrants from France and elsewhere, who created a housing shortage and raised the cost of living: at the same time their presence further weakened the local orientation of Geneva.

The ministers in Geneva also enjoyed, from the beginning, another advantage. Because the town had achieved self-government so recently, they did not have to deal with an experienced and respected civic body, conscious of old prerogatives and traditional authority and with a long record of success in the preservation of public order. The ruling group in Geneva consisted of an insecure body of relative newcomers to political responsibility. They were threatened not only by the old claims of Savoy but also by the new demands of Bern, without whose armies it is doubtful that there would have

[33]These details are worked out by Emile G. Léonard, *Histoire générale du Protestantisme,* 3 vols. (Paris: Presses Universitaires de France, 1961-64), 1:281-82.

[34]Robert M. Kingdon, "Was the Protestant Reformation a Revolution? The Case of Geneva," *Studies in Church History* 12 (1975): 203-22

[35]It is also of some significance, in this connection, that they spoke a language which could be readily understood outside Geneva, as a local clergy could not have done; the language of Geneva, as Höpfl, *Christian Polity of Calvin,* 135, has described it, was "a Savoyard patois containing substantial admixtures of German."

been a Genevan Reformation.[36] They must also have been, for the most part, uninformed, doubtful, and apprehensive about whatever religious settlement might lie ahead.

Nevertheless the situation in Geneva did not differ sufficiently from the situation elsewhere to make the victory of the ministers over the magistrates easy. Indeed, Calvin's own understanding of the relations between civic and spiritual authority always attributed, though with much ambiguity, a large responsibility to the civil magistrate in the administration of the church. Although candidates for the ministry in Geneva were proposed by the ministers, they had to be approved, and continued to be appointed, by the council; Calvin himself was appointed through this procedure. On the other hand the Genevan magistrates, unusually conscious, perhaps, of their lack of learning, made no effort to interfere with the decisions of the ministers – as occurred in Bern as well as Strasbourg – on matters of doctrine.[37]

The most serious source of friction between magistrates and ministers in Calvin's Geneva was the unwillingness of the populace, including many who had participated enthusiastically in the iconoclastic disorders of 1535, to submit to the spiritual and moral disciplines the ministers proposed to enforce. The resistance of the Genevans to clerical control found expression in an anonymous note of protest attached to the pulpit of one of the Genevan churches. It called the attention of the magistrates to the fact that "people did not wish to have so many masters," and that the ministers "had now gone far enough in their course of censure."[38] An open letter exhorted the council not to be "ruled by the voice or the will of one man, for you see that men have many and divers opinions: each one wants to be governed as he likes."[39] Resistance also found expression in "daily clamors" of protest against actions of the consistory that interrupted sermons, Calvin's included.[40] "Unclean spirits," he reported, were seeking "any sort of pretext to overthrow the authority of the church."[41]

In dealing with this problem, Calvin found the support of the magistrates singularly unreliable; the council was likely to fall into "a tumult for no reason," he declared; they were so incapable of initiative "in a good and praiseworthy cause" and "so childish that they are frightened by a silly shake

---

[36]As even Eire, *War Against the Idols*, 124, recognizes. Robert M. Kingdon, "Was the Protestant Reformation a Revolution?" has argued that Geneva's Reformation was a revolution because it involved the overthrow of a traditional and legitimate ruling class, i.e. the Duke of Savoy and the clergy headed by the bishop. I am much indebted to this work; but in my reading of these events, it would be more accurate to say that Geneva's revolution produced its Reformation.

[37]Cf. Calvin's letter to Viret, August 23, 1542 (*CO*, 11: 431).

[38]Text in *CO*, 11:546, n. 8.

[39]Text in *CO*, 12:564.

[40]Calvin to Viret, March 27, 1547, *CO*, 12:505.

[41]Letter to Myconius, March 14, 1542, *CO*, 11:379.

of the head,"[42] a characterization that suggests their political incompetence as well as their resistance to Calvin's policies. The ministers seemed to him almost completely isolated. "The crushing effect of a general though false consensus against us," he confessed, "is a hard temptation and one almost impossible to resist."[43] He could only console himself – he was often given to such comparisons – by reflecting that "greater commotions had been stirred up against Moses and the prophets, although they had to govern the people of God."[44] This might be taken to imply that Calvin considered the Genevans the people of some other ruler. But it also suggests the universal context in which Calvin placed the quite local problems of Geneva.

The tension between Calvin and Geneva came into focus in a dispute about the right to excommunicate, a sensitive matter where excommunication had long served the needs of social control as well as of spiritual discipline. In other Protestant communities, the right to excommunicate had been retained by the magistrates and was little exercised; in Geneva alone it was substantially taken over by the ministers. After festering for more than a decade, controversy over this matter reached a climax in the early 1550s, when the power of Calvin's opponents was increasing and the council resisted, with renewed vigor, the right of the ministers to excommunicate. "You cannot believe how much I am displeased with the present state of our republic," Calvin wrote early in 1551.[45] A year later he complained again, "Our fellow citizens occasion us much concern; the disorder of this republic is so great that the church of God is tossed about like Noah's ark in the waters of the deluge."[46] The situation was still unchanged in 1553: his enemies still strove "to overthrow the whole order and condition of the republic."[47] He blamed the opposition less on licentiousness itself, for this could be controlled by appropriate institutional measures, than on men who, seeking power for themselves, encouraged it.[48] This confrontation between Calvin and his adversaries in Geneva may help to explain the trial and execution of Servetus, which occurred when tensions were at their height; each side needed to demonstrate its zeal for orthodoxy.

[42]Letter to Viret, March 27, 1547, *CO,* 12:505.

[43]Comm. Matt. 26:10.

[44]Letter to the faithful in France, July 24, 1547, *CO,* 12:562.

[45]Letter to Viret, January 24, 1551, *CO,* 14:27.

[46]Letter to Blaurer, February 14, 1552, *CO,* 14:474.

[47]Letter to Christopher Fabri, January 13, 1553, *CO,* 14:455.

[48]Letter to Bullinger, November 26, 1553, *CO,* 14:673-74.

Calvin did so by the arrest and prosecution of Servetus, the magistrates by the hideous manner of his execution.[49]

The situation remained tense until May of 1555, when Calvin's opponents overreached themselves and the tide turned in his favor.[50] Although the dispute was not resolved in any formal way, the magistrates generally accepted excommunication by the consistory, and the number of excommunications rapidly increased.[51]

It is somewhat ironical, therefore, that Calvin never considered the situation secure. Two years later, he wrote Farel, "Besides open contentions, you will not believe how many ambushes and clandestine intrigues Satan daily directs against us. So, though public order is tranquil, not everyone can enjoy repose." There were still "many hidden enemies at home, some of them eager to come out in the open."[52] In one of his last works, composed when he knew that his death was near, he was still anxious about the security of his work in Geneva. "Today," he reflected, "the authority of God's servants, whom he has furnished with excellent and wonderful gifts, protects and preserves the church. But once they are dead, a sad deterioration will promptly begin, and impiety now hidden will erupt without restraint."[53] He had built far better than he could believe.

The extent of his triumph is suggested by the contrast between post-Reformation Geneva and post-Reformation Basel and Strasbourg. This hardly requires elaborate demonstration: for the difference in atmosphere it is sufficient to mention Servetus, whom Geneva burned, and Castellio, who retreated from Geneva to Basel. Geneva was not at all afflicted with the ambivalence of Basel and Strasbourg toward the rival claims of Swiss and Saxon theology. Calvin felt strong enough to maintain his independence from both Zwingli and Luther, although, while remaining on good terms with both Melanchthon and Bullinger, he preferred Lutheran to Zwinglian theology. Nor could Geneva tolerate the religious diversity that persisted till the latter part of the century in Basel and Strasbourg. This difference is largely the consequence of the ascendancy in Geneva of an alien and embattled clergy, whose consciousness of their own authority and whose

---

[49]Cf. his letter to Farel, August 20, 1553, *CO*, 14:589-90. His letter to Sulzer, September 8, 1553, *CO*, 14:614-15, suggests the effect on him of the capital executions of his own followers in France; he thought it appropriate that the saints should display no less zeal than their adversaries. The zeal of the magistrates against Servetus does not, of course, imply the fervor of their *Protestantism*.

[50]Monter, *Geneva*, 75-88, provides a clear and succinct account of the entire episode. Calvin treated it most fully in a letter to Bullinger, June 15, 1555, *CO*, 15:676-85.

[51]Lewis, "Calvinism in Time of Calvin and Beza," 50; Kingdon, "Was the Protestant Reformation a Revolution?" 218, citing the statistics of Walther Köhler, *Züricher Ehegericht und Genfer Konsistorium*, 2 vols. (Leipzig: Heinsius Nachfolger, 1932-42), 2:614, n. 544.

[52]February 3, 1557, *CO*, 16:406.

[53]Comm. Josh. 24:29.

willingness to resort in practice to authoritarian measures had been stimulated by struggle with the magistrates.[54] The results of their success in this struggle are implicit in John Knox's description of Geneva as "the maist perfyt schoole of Chryst that ever was in the erth since the dayis of the Apostillis."[55]

On the other hand, Geneva, so impoverished before the Reformation in the matter of the learned culture that had collaborated in bringing on the Reformation in Basel and Strasbourg, started, *after* its Reformation, to become a center of learning. In the *Ecclesiastical Ordinances* of 1541, Calvin had recognized the need for a school such as Geneva had never possessed, not only to instruct potential ministers "in the languages and humanities" but also "for instructing children for civil government." Busy as he was otherwise, and inhabiting a town so culturally deprived, it took him nearly two decades to fulfill this plan, which brought to Geneva an academy on the model of Sturm's *gymnasium* in which Calvin had taught in Strasbourg between 1538 and 1541. Ironically, however, it seems to have trained few local students, at least for the ministry. And it was *because* of the Reformation that Geneva became a printing center. With the influx of French refugees in the 1550s, the number of printers and booksellers in Geneva rose from fewer than ten to over three hundred, among them the distinguished Paris printer Robert Estienne. Geneva replaced Antwerp as the principal center of Bible printing in Europe.[56] Because of her backwardness, the Reformation in Geneva had differed crucially from the Reformation in other cities. But because of her Reformation, she had, in some respects, caught up with them.

[54]Cf. the observations of Michael Mullett, *Radical Religious Movements in Early Modern Europe* (London: Allen & Unwin, 1980), 64-65, on the deviations of Calvinism from later medieval lay spirituality.

[55]Quoted by A. G. Dickens, *The English Reformation* (London: Batsford, 1964), 198.

[56]Elizabeth L. Eisenstein, *The Printing Press as an Agent of Change*, 2 vols. (New York: Cambridge University Press, 1979), 1:206, 328, 410; Monter, *Geneva*, 5, 166.

Anti-Calvinist Broadsheet

"A Calvinist presentation, in which human Reason and the arrogant Calvinists, with the philosophical arguments by which they try to explain the Divine Mysteries, arrive by stagecoach and destroy themselves colliding with the cornerstone of Zion. Issued for the relief of all the saddened and attacked Christians of Lower Hesse."

III

Popular Culture

Jewish Magic in Early Modern Germany

R. Po-chia Hsia*

ONE ASPECT OF JEWISH MAGIC, the attribution of blood magic to Jews by Christians in late medieval and early modern Europe, is the subject of this essay. The first part constructs a discourse of ritual murder, on the basis of analyzing extant documents generated by ritual murder trials and accusations in the Holy Roman Empire between 1450 and 1560. Judicial transcripts, pamphlets, broadsheets, woodcuts, songsheets, carnival plays, and theological treatises served as sources for reconstructing this ritual murder discourse. The second part discusses reasons for the decline of ritual murder trials and the forces undermining the unity of ritual murder discourse in the middle decades of the sixteenth century. The final part of the essay traces the legacy of the blood libel for Protestants, Catholics, and Jews in early modern Germany.

The Discourse

In a supposed ritual murder, one or several Jews were accused of kidnapping and murdering Christian children, almost always boys, in order to seek revenge on Christians, but more especially to use their blood for magical purposes, in the preparation of poison, for circumcision, for Passover service, for the ritual purification of rabbis, for stopping menstrual and other kinds of bleeding.[1]

We can clearly distinguish a structure of the blood libel by analyzing it as a discourse, in which various social voices made use of the ensemble of religious, political, and magical vocabulary to contest and define the nature of social reality. The three levels of this structure began with an initial process of rumor or gossip, when a Christian heard about the need of blood on the part of the Jews and made an attempt to sell it to them, or when the corpse of a child was discovered, or actually when a murder had just been committed. This initial process can be described as the appropriation of an immemorial myth – one transmitted by folk songs and tales, by pictorial depiction, pilgrimages, and shrines – namely, that Jews had murdered Christian children in the past, and that blood played a central role in Jewish magic; it activated oral legends about Jews and applied them toward the explanation or resolution of an immediate problem in daily life.

---

*This was given in November 1987 and anticipates some of the arguments of my book, *The Myth of Ritual Murder: Jews and Magic in Reformation Germany* (New Haven: Yale University Press, 1988).

[1]See Hermann L. Strack, *The Jew and Human Sacrifice*, trans. Henry Blanchamp (New York: Bloch, 1909), *passim.*

The second level of a ritual murder discourse moved from accusation to interrogation. Here, the murmurs and whispers of village gossip became submerged in the official voice of the judicial apparatus and the protestations of the suspects. The interlocution was an uneven one, as the magistrates called in witnesses, weighed the evidence, and applied torture, while the Jews tried steadfastly to maintain their innocence. At this stage, the discourse became a political one as well: friends and relatives of the suspects appealed to imperial authorities; city councils exchanged queries and warnings about other possible ritual murders; and there was often a contestation of judicial competence, because many of the Jews were under imperial jurisdiction. If the evidence proved inconclusive, or when the real causes of the murders came to light, the Jews were set free. But too often the Jews were forced to admit their alleged guilt under judicial torture, thus retroactively confirming the initial rumor of ritual murder.

The third and final level was the sentencing and public execution of the Jews. Banished were the discordant voices of unequal contestation in the process of interrogation: the "crime" had been confessed to; the voice of the evildoers was muted; replacing the cacophony of angry accusation, stern interrogation, and tormented protestations was the chorus of unison. Now, the discourse resounded in the voice of a vindicated and triumphant Christian community. The public execution itself served as a dramatic representation of the "evil" of Jews and the triumph of Christianity: folk songs and tales were composed; eyewitness accounts were written down and sold in cheap flysheets and pamphlets; entries were recorded in chronicles; and in the case of the 1470 Endingen trial, a morality play was composed to commemorate the Christian triumph over Jews.[2]

These alleged ritual murders shared certain characteristics: the victims were usually pre-pubescent boys; their corpses showed signs of torture, sometimes prick marks, dismemberment, or wounds similar to the crucifixion; the ritualistic shedding of blood supposedly played a central role in the murder.

The structure of ritual murder discourse resembles a pyramid in that a broad base of popular legends and folk tales provided the universal grammar for the articulation of more specific forms of antisemitic language. I have chosen to call this "popular culture" without restricting the currency of these ideas to only the lower social groups. The fact that these beliefs functioned as myths implied that they constituted the common cultural universe for society. Out of this common expectation about Jews as magicians and their need for Christian blood arose incidents in which Jews came under suspicion. Once they were denounced to the authorities, the realm of popular discourse and magical beliefs interacted with the realm of legal discourse and politics. Depending on the judicial outcome and the political pressure surrounding a

---

[2]See Karl von Amira, ed., *Das Endinger Judenspiel* (Halle: Niemeyer, 1883).

trial, the case would either be resolved at this level or transformed into an execution. The process from accusation to interrogation to execution would be like the ascension of a pyramid; out of the many potential cases only a few actually resulted in executions.

Two crucial components underlie the structure of ritual murder discourse: the role of magic in popular religion, and the tensions between a learned religion and traditions of folk beliefs in Christian society. As Marcel Mauss suggests in his *General Theory of Magic*, a magician is not really a free agent; he is forced to play out a role assigned to him by tradition or defined by the needs of his clients. In Reformation Germany, the needs of the common folk created the roles which were then enforced on reluctant Jewish "actors": they were to play the part of magicians, be it as fortune-tellers, finders of lost objects, makers of amulets, or, in these alleged crimes, as ritualistic murderers. If we understand one of the central functions of magic as the fulfillment of the gap between wish and reality, then the magical role forced upon Jews in ritual murders can be understood as the need by pre-Reformation German society to create an immediate salvific presence. It provided a discursive outlet for the unspeakable crimes committed against children, be it infanticide, or child murders, perhaps sexual in origin, or resulting from the domestic violence of late medieval society. It disguised the real event by creating an alternative explanatory model of a dialectical opposition between the two binary opposites of Jew/magician/murderer and Christian/believer/victim, between black, demonic magic and lifegiving, godly religion. At a deeper level, it produced a powerful experience of sacrifice which was central to the self-expression of late medieval piety in a century of the imitation of Christ and the many moving and gruesome depictions of the crucifixion. In a ritual murder discourse two sacrifices were involved: by torturing and murdering a Christian boy, the Jews were reenacting the crucifixion, giving it a salvific immediacy and power which the Mass could not rival; by exposing the "crimes" of the Jews and avenging the "murder," sacrificing the evildoers to an offended deity, the triumph of Christianity was celebrated and the crucifixion of Jesus avenged and vindicated. A ritual murder was an imitation of Christ par excellence; both the *Judenspiel* of Endingen, which commemorated the 1462 "murder," and the *Passionspiel* of Freiburg, performed on Corpus Christi Day, drew from a common structure of ideas and events, represented by a similar dramatic conception, and reflected the obsession with sacrifice.

The explicit connections between the crucifixion and ritual murder accusations were also manifest in the writings of the learned theologian Johann Eck, Luther's chief opponent during the early Reformation years. In the wake of the 1529 Pösing ritual murder trial, the reformer in Nürnberg, Andreas Osiander, composed an anonymous defense of the Jews, denying the reality of ritual murders.[3] In 1540, when another ritual murder charge was raised against the Jews in Sappenfeld, Eck wrote *Refutation of a Jewish Booklet* in which he explained that Jews needed Christian blood in order to wash away their own bloodstains which God had inflicted on them because they had crucified Christ.[4] He concluded that "it is no wonder that the Jews now buy the blood of innocent children, just as their fathers bought the innocent blood of Jesus Christ from Judas with thirty pennies."[5] In a tone charged with emotion, Eck relates his own personal experience: in 1504, when he went as a young student from Cologne to the University of Freiburg, he witnessed a ritual murder case. A father in the village of Waldkirch near Freiburg sold his son to two Jews because they wanted some blood; he didn't know they were going to kill him. The two Jews were arrested and brought to trial in Freiburg. Eck described how the small corpse was bled white and pale; that he saw and touched the wounds of the boy with his own hands.[6] The child could have become a saint just as Simon of Trent had been blessed, and his corpse would have been a relic bestowing salvific merit to those who beheld and touched, if not for the fact that the Jews refused to confess under repeated torture and had to be let go, after repeated orders from Emperor Maximilian I.[7]

Christian blood could wash away the stains of blood on the Jews, so Eck argued. It reflected the fundamentally magical mental structure of an educated doctor of theology and university professor in early sixteenth-century Germany. It was sympathetic magic at work: opposites attract one another, and a sympathetic substance forced the other out; thus Jews needed Christian blood to cleanse their own bloodstains from Christ.[8] The potency of blood in a ritual murder discourse derived from the fact that it was spilled from a sacrificial victim. Sacrifice, death, and magic formed a continuum in this mental world. Magic was power. And one could find a host of legends in Germanic folklore concerning the power of blood: it

---

[3]The anonymously published tract was republished by Moritz Stern, who correctly identified the author; see *Andreas Osianders Schrift über die Blutbeschuldigung*, ed. Moritz Stern (Kiel: Fiencke, 1893).

[4]Johann Eck, *Ains Judenbüchlins Verlegung: darin ain Christ / gantzer Christenhait zu schmach / will es geschehe den Juden unrecht in bezichtigung der Christen kinder mordt* (Ingolstadt: Alexander Weissenhorn, 1541), sig. J4r-K1r. For a brief description of the polemics between Eck and Osiander, see Heinrich Graetz, *Geschichte der Juden von den ältesten Zeiten bis auf die Gegenwart*, 11 vols (Leipzig: Leimer, 1891-1911), 9:309-11.

[5]"Nit ist zu verwundern: dz die juden jetzt kaufen das blut der unschuldigen kinder, so ir väter kauft haben das unschuldig blut IHESU Christ vm 30. pfennig von Judas." Ibid., sig. K2r.

[6]Ibid., sig B3v-4v.

[7]Stadtarchiv Freiburg A1XII C, nos. 28 and 29 for the correspondence on the trial; for the confessions of the Jews, see Ratsprotocol 1504 B5 (P) XIIIa, no. 9, fols. 4v-5r.

[8]On sympathetic magic, see Marcel Mauss, *A General Theory of Magic* (New York: Norton, 1975), 72.

healed diseases, stopped bleeding, and spellbound reluctant lovers.[9] Violent death created magical power, and in the late sixteenth century the Rhenish physician Johann Weyer recorded many examples of folk beliefs in infanticide and witchcraft which were similar to ritual murder legends.[10]

A sacrifice, performed in a magical or religious rite, is essentially a coercive act: either the victim is an unwilling one, or the deity is forced into manifesting his divine power in exchange for the sacrificial gift.[11] Through the double sacrifice in a ritual murder discourse, a Christian community cleansed itself of a polluting element, namely the magicians, Jewish murderers, and coerced God to manifest his divine power in response. The idea of religious contamination was reflected in the symbols and metaphors of folk literature of the time. The identification of feces with demonic pollution is well known in Luther's writings; his scatology, in fact, reflected the symbolic structures of popular culture. In the popular folk tales of the peasant rogue Til Ulenspiegel, the crafty peasant tricked some Frankfurt Jews into buying his own feces as medicine (story 35); Thomas Murner, Luther's Franciscan foe, lampooned the reformer with literary and pictorial feces;[12] in the poem *Of Jewish Honor*, published anonymously in 1571, the poet chanted that Jews should not be tolerated because their very presence polluted the purity of Christian communities.[13] And what was purer in a community than its children? The alleged child murders by Jews were particularly horrendous to late medieval Germans because of the identification of their ideal family life with the image of a holy kinship (*der heilige Sippe*), with Joseph, Mary, and the baby Jesus.[14]

As I have argued earlier, a sacrifice is essentially an exchange; and in response to this ritual murder discourse, God was supposed to manifest his salvific grace. Reports of miracles followed upon the convictions and executions of Jews in these trials. In the 1540 Sappenfeld case, the sacrificial and miraculous nature of the death showed itself in a subsequent folk song.

[9]See Handwörterbuch des Deutschen Aberglaubens, 10 vols., ed. Hanns Bächtold-Stäubli and Eduard Hoffmann-Krayer (Berlin: De Gruyter, 1927-42), *s.v.* "Blut," cc. 1434-42; and Lynn Thorndike, *A History of Magic and Experimental Science,* 8 vols. (New York: Macmillan, 1923-58), 5:101-2, 462, 602, 639, 660; 6:240, 243, 292, 484.

[10]Johann Weyer, *De praestigiis daemonum: Von Teuffelsgespenst, Zauberern und Grifftbereytern, Schwarzkünstlern, Hexen und Unholden . . .* (Frankfurt: Nicolaus Basseum, 1586), Bk. 3, chap. 4, p. 152; for folk recipes using blood to stop bleeding, see pp. 311-12.

[11]Marcel Mauss, *The Gift: Forms and Functions of Exchange in Archaic Societies,* trans. Ian Cunnison (London: Coehn & West, 1969).

[12]See his "Von den Grossen Lutherischen Narren," in *Thomas Murners Deutsche Schriften,* ed. Paul Merker (Strasbourg, 1918), 9:267

[13]*Der Iuden Erbarkeit* (n.d., 1571), sig. B2v. In her book, *Purity and Danger: An Analysis of Concepts of Pollution and Taboo* (London: Routledge & Kegan Paul, 1966), Mary Douglas argues that the fear of religious pollution is fundamental in delineating religious communities.

[14]John Bossy, *Christianity in the West, 1400-1700,* (New York: Oxford University Press, 1985), 10-11.

It narrates how the Jews tortured the boy for three days, piercing his ears, castrating him, cutting off his fingers and toes, stabbing him all over, and cutting three crosses on his body. More revealing was the alleged event after the execution of the Jews. The corpse of the infant boy was put on display, and five weeks later it bled, showing God's mercy, so says the song.[15] The bleeding Eucharist was the central element in a purported host desecration and one of the most powerful salvific images of pre-Reformation piety. The complete confusion of images between Christ and the child, between the Eucharist and the corpse, created an immediate salvific presence "showing God's mercy" to the authorities and peasants of Sappenfeld. It was nothing less than a eucharistic sacrifice, a social Mass, enacted in a discourse: the language was drawn in part from church liturgy and in part from the vocabulary of popular magic; the interlocutors encompassed the Christian community and the "other"; the result reaffirmed the unity and boundary of the collectivity and the reassurance of God's grace. Miracles, apparitions, healings, the erection of shrines, the beginning of pilgrimage were all signs of the divine response to this double sacrifice. The benefit to the commmunity was more than spiritual; pilgrimage brought a temporary prosperity to the locality. Seen from one perspective of the evangelical movement, folk superstitions and greed went hand in hand. Osiander accused greedy monks and priests of fabricating the myth of ritual murders. In investigating these charges, a magistrate must ask himself, Osiander cautioned, "whether the priests or monks were not themselves eager to obtain the appearance of greater sanctitiy, more miracles, and to establish new pilgrimages, or whether they were much inclined to exterminate the Jews."[16]

Ritual murder discourse narrated the role of Jews as evil magicians, but the translation of legend into trial and execution depended upon the cooperation of the elite. In other words, popular belief in magic alone cannot explain the escalation of magical discourse from legend to interrogation; moreover, many ordinary Christians went to Jews for fortune-telling and medicine. Obviously, magic and Jewish magicians played an ambiguous role for Christians; they could heal as well as kill. It was really the confluence of a particular event and the participation of the elite in a universe of magic which precipitated the escalation of the levels of discourse. The crucial element leading to a trial and persecution was the displacement of a legal discourse by a magical discourse: all these cases were heard by secular authorities, few with training in civil and canon law. Paradoxically, for the

---

[15]*Ein hübsch new lied von Zweyen Juden / vnd einem Kind / zu Sappenfelt newlich geschehen* (n.p., n.d.), sig. F3-3v.

[16]Stern, ed., *Osianders . . . über die Blutbeschuldigung*, 42, ". . . ob nicht pfaffen/ oder munch da selbst/ den schein grosser heyligkeyt zu erlangen/ grosse wunderwerck/ vnd newe walfarten an zu richten/ begirig/ oder sunst die Juden zu vertilgen seer geneygt weren."

magistrates and clerks, the crucial question was not one of the unconscious subtext of magic, but the language of common law, which functioned to articulate and mask a myth, and read more like a liturgical, dramatic text than a legal document. The 1470 Endingen trial record was copied down in the Freiburg *Kopialbuch,* a compilation and a copybook of the texts of all the privileges accorded to the city. When the Freiburg city fathers were confronted with a purported ritual murder case in 1504, they could rely not only on living memory of the Endinger trial but also on the actual, authentic judicial proceedings thirty-four years past.

There are three important conclusions we can draw from an analysis of these ritual murder discourses. First, they represented attempts to fabricate and sustain a myth: that Jews were black magicians and Christians their innocent victims, and that God would ultimately vindicate their sacrifice and expose these "crimes." The function of the myth in fact masked the real motives behind some of the accusations, be it a personal grievance by a Christian debtor against a Jewish moneylender, or a general hatred of Jews, or a need to explain a gruesome murder, or a desire by the local clergy and authorities to create a moment of sanctity and fame. Crucial were not the real events or non-events behind the discourse but the representations. Second, for Christians, these discourses represented triumphs and vindications in the battle against false religion. Suspicions arose always around Easter, when the conjunction of Passover and the commemoration of the passion of Christ created powerful emotions. The accusations demonstrated to the Christians that the crucifixion was not only a historical, unrepeatable event, but a recurring tragedy or "crime," perpetrated even by the Jews of the Holy Roman Empire. Its recurrence was thus both a source of passion and sorrow and a comfort because of the ritualistic, hence repeatable and reliable, nature of the sacrifice. For German society on the eve of the Reformation, these discourses meant nothing less than the triumph of true religion over false magic. Finally, looking at ritual murder and host desecration discourses from our perspective, they were indeed magical representations, but the magic was performed by Christians, not by the accused Jews. A double sacrifice, a twofold rite, transformed reluctant Jews into magicians, and then destroyed their malevolent "magic" by a powerful ritual of Christian sacrifice and exorcism, in which, quite literally, the communities were cleansed of magical pollution and became, so to speak, *Judenfrei.*

Suppression

The fabrication of myth and the battle against Jewish magic were not confined to late medieval Christianity alone. These efforts continued through the first decades of the Reformation in Germany, under a different ecclesiastical leadership, a new system of theology and rites, using new strategies to disenchant the Christian community of magical possession.

No one embodied the ambivalence toward magic more vividly than Luther himself; he both believed in it and condemned it. Especially toward his latter years, Luther was preoccupied with the malevolent forces of magic, particularly that of the Jews. In *On the Ineffable Name of God* (1543), a work which attacks the cabala as mere superstition and magic, Luther exclaims that "a Jew fabricates as much idolatry and magic as the hair on nine cows, that is, countless and infinite."[17] He had believed for some time that Jews were poisoners, influenced most probably by legends of well poisonings by Jews prior to the Black Death.[18] For Luther, the "Jewish danger" was the product of a mind which placed true, evangelical Christianity on one side, and all opponents of the reform, real or imaginary, on the other. Thus he attacks Jews, papists, and Turks in one breath in *Of the Jews and Their Lies* (1543);[19] they were all idolators, blind believers in the false religion of the flesh and of the law, whereas the evangelicals trusted in the vital religion of the spirit. The binary opposition between old and new law, flesh and spirit, superstition (*Aberglaube*) and faith (*Glaube*), magic and religion resulted in a renewed and stricter attempt to define the boundaries of the sacral community. Jews were assigned a prominent role as the quintessential *other* in Luther's social and psychological drama of salvation.

The need to delineate a new community of evangelical Christians was particularly acute in the early Reformation years because opponents of the reform accused the movement of being instigated by the Jews. When Osiander ventured to publish an anonymous tract defending Jews against the charge of ritual murder, Eck called him the "evangelical scoundrel" (*evangelisch lumpen*) who dared to defend the "bloodthirsty Jews."[20] The Lutherans, Eck curses on, were all evil monks who had stirred up the Peasants' War and were now defending the archenemies of Christendom.[21] Host desecrations by Jews were no different from the Lutheran desecration of the eucharistic sacrament.[22] Eck concludes his long-winded vituperation by accusing Osiander of slander against the whole of Christianity because by denying the truth of ritual murders, the evangelical reformer was in essence accusing Christians of murder, magic, and lies.[23]

---

[17]*D. Martin Luthers Werke. Kritische Gesamtausgabe* (Weimar: Böhlau, 1883–), 53:602. Hereafter cited as *WA, WA BR (Briefwechsel)* or *WA TR (Tischreden)*.

[18]*WA BR* 3:821.On legends of well poisonings prior to the Black Death, see for example, Heinrich Schreiber, ed., *Urkundenbuch der Stadt Freiburg im Breisgau,* 2 vols. (Freiburg im Breisgau: Herder, 1828-29), 1:379-83.

[19]*WA* 53:542, 544.

[20]Eck, *Ains Judenbüchlin Verlegung,* sig. A4.

[21]Ibid., sig. N4v-O1v.

[22]Ibid., sig. V4.

[23]Ibid., sig. Z4-4v.

Marcel Mauss characterizes a magical system as consisting of three elements – a system of representation, of rites, and of practitioners. Through these concepts we can better understand the strategies employed by the Reformation to disenchant Christianity of magical possession by the Jews. The first method of disenchantment was the dissection and appropriation of the magical system of representation, namely, the Christian appropriation of Hebrew.[24] Another approach was the study or exposition of the rites of Judaism. Finally, the practitioners of magic, the Jews themselves, were rendered harmless by confinement in ghettos or by expulsions.

A magical language consists of signs and symbols accessible only to a small circle of practitioners and hence is a closely guarded secret. Its very power lies not in the meaning of the text but in the coercive force of the incantations and magical formulae. Magic enabled one to cheat even the crafty Jews, as the legend of Faust offered an example of the black magician cutting off his own leg as a collateral to a Jewish usurer and winning back more than his share of wealth in the end.[25] While a handful of Christian scholars avidly learned Hebrew in order to read cabalistic books, in order to gain access into the mystical, magical world of ultimate knowledge of the divine, the common people did not hesitate to procure amulets and talismans inscribed with Hebrew letters.[26] When a visitation of the Saxon parishes turned up amulets, Luther bitterly denounced the village pastors, still clinging to their old ways and beliefs, and in whose possession were found magical books with spells, charms, prayers, and names of angels and demons written in Hebrew.[27]

For Luther, the attack on Catholic superstitions paralleled the campaign to unmask Jewish magic as mere superstitions. To unmask, to expose, one has to know the language of one's opponents. While a defender of the old faith like Eck attacked the Lutherans for insisting the study of Hebrew was essential for recovering the true Christian faith,[28] for the Wittenberger and many evangelical clerics, knowledge of the Old Testament in its original represented a rescue of the true Christian heritage from rabbinic glossators and Jewish captivity. It was the only way to break the spell of a magical

---

[24]For a succinct introduction to the history of Hebrew learning by Christians in Germany, see Otto Kluge, "Die hebräische Sprachwissenschaft in Deutschland im Zeitalter des Humanismus," *Zeitschrift für die Geschichte der Juden in Deutschland* 3 (1931): 81-97, 180-93.

[25]See *Historia von D. Johann Fausten dem Weitbeschreyten Zauberer und Schwarzkünstler,* ed. Richard Benz (Stuttgart: Reclam, 1977), 81-83.

[26]On Christian Hebraica, see Jerome Friedman, *The Most Ancient Testimony: Sixteenth Century Christian-Hebraica in the Age of Renaissance Nostalgia* (Athens, Ohio: Ohio University Press, 1983). For the history and preparation of Hebrew amulets, see T. Schrire, *Hebrew Amulets: Their Decipherment and Interpretation* (London: Routledge & Kegan Paul, 1966), esp. 69-72 on Christian-Hebrew amulets and the use of Hebrew inscriptions by Christians.

[27]"Vom Schem Hamphoras," *WA* 53:614.

[28]Eck, *Ains Judenbüchlin Verlegung,* sig. P4v-Q2v.

language, and through its appropriation, evangelical Christianity would triumph over Jews and Catholics.

Once a magical language is dissected and studied, it loses its force of enchantment. Furthermore, the knowledge of Hebrew made possible a better understanding of Jewish liturgy and helped to dispel the mystery surrounding Passover service, which had sustained many ritual murder and host desecration suspicions. The writings of Johannes Pfefferkorn provide a most instructive example. He composed two tracts to explain to Christians the observance of the Sabbath and the Passover: *A Booklet on Jewish Confession* (1508) and *Explication on how Jews observe Passover* (1509).[29] While one of the aims of these tracts was to expose Jewish superstitions and "blasphemies" against Christianity, Pfefferkorn was careful to show that they were not magical rites in which Jews slaughtered Christian children. In an earlier work exhorting the Jews to convert, Pfefferkorn refuted the legend believed by "the vulgar Christians" that Jews needed Christian blood; if one by chance came across Jews who murder Christian children, it was out of hatred and not magical necessity.[30]

Whereas Pfefferkorn merely described the celebration of Sabbath and Passover, another convert, Anton Margaritha, the son of the chief rabbi in Regensburg, baptized in 1521, translated the entirety of the the prayer book used by the Jewish communities in early sixteenth-century Germany.[31] The only place where magic is mentioned is when Margaritha laments the cabala and the magic of the Jews, superstitions which did not help them for "there is no people who gets run over, robbed, and killed more often on the open roads than Jews."[32] *Der gantz Jüdisch Glaub* exerted a profound influence on the evaluation of Jews by the new Lutheran church: Luther read it, praised

[29]*Eyn buchlijn der iudenbeicht* (Cologne: Johann von Landen, 1508); there were also a Latin and a Low German edition published by Landen in 1508: *Libellus de Judaica confessione sive sabbato afflictionis* and *Eyn biochelgyn der ioeden bicht.* The tract on Passover is *Explicatio quomodo ceci illi iudei suum pascha servent: et maxime quo ritu paschalem eam cenam manducent* (Cologne: Heinrich von Nussia, 1509).

[30]Johannes Pfefferkorn. *Speculum adhortationis iudaice ad Christum* (Speyer: C. Hist, 1507); reprinted by M. von Werden of Cologne in 1508. See sig. D1-1v: "Dicitur vulgo inter christianos Judeis necessario opus esse uti sanguine christiano ad medelam propterea eos occidere infantulos christianos: ad hoc eos feda quadam egritudine laborare. Charissimi christiani nolite his adhibere fidem . . . redibile est inventos esse et fortasse adhuc inveniri posse iudeos, qui christianorum infantes ad necem clam sectentur non propter sanguinis habendi inde necessitatem, sed odii et ultionis causa in christianos."

[31]See Anthonius Margaritha, *Der Gantz Jüdisch Glaub mit sampt eyner grundtlichtenn und warhafftigen anzeygunge, aller satzungen, Ceremonien, gebetten, heymliche und offentliche gebreuch, deren sich die Juden halten, durch das gantz Jar. . . .* (Augsburg: Heinrich Steiner, 1531). For Margaritha himself, see Josef Mieses, *Die älteste gedruckte deutsche übersetzung des jüdischen Gebetbuchs aus dem Jahre 1530 und ihr Autor Antonius Margaritha* (Vienna: Löwit, 1916); for the conflict between Margaritha and the Jewish communities, see Selma Stern-Taeubler, *Josel of Rosheim, Commander of Jewry in the Holy Roman Empire,* trans. Gertrude Hirschler (Philadelphia: Jewish Publication Society of America, 1965).

[32]Margaritha, *Der Gantz Jüdisch Glaub,* sig. Y4v.

it, and was confirmed in his belief that both Jews and Catholics were superstitious and believed in good works.[33] After the first Augsburg edition of 1530, it was reprinted once in 1531 in Augsburg, at least three times in Frankfurt (1544, 1561, 1689), and in 1731 in Leipzig; it provided the standard text for introducing Lutheran pastors to the customs and ceremonies of the Jews.[34] The exposition of Jewish rites aimed at knowledge over an alien religion; it resulted in the mastery and ridicule of what was once an unknown magical system. Jewish magic was now transformed into Jewish superstition.

The final attack on Jewish magic concentrated on suppressing the practitioners. From the 1450s to 1521, town after town in the Holy Roman Empire expelled their Jews; by the mid-sixteenth century, only the two imperial cities of Frankfurt and Worms had any important Jewish communities.[35] Economic and political considerations stood behind many of these expulsions. Usury was the universal charge; and the fact that citizens of imperial cities got entangled in legal disputes with Jews under the protection of princes and lords, who were often hostile to civic freedom, moved the city fathers to expel Jews. In the fourteen years before the magistrates of Nürnberg expelled the Jewish community in 1498, they registered over 23,000 civil cases related to Jews; all of them arose from moneylending, in addition to criminal investigations regarding stolen goods pawned to Jews.[36]

---

[33]*WA Tr* 5:5504.

[34]The 1544 Frankfurt edition was published by C. Egenolff; the 1713 Leipzig edition by Friedrich Lanckischen. The Leipzig edition has a foreword by Magister Christian Reineccius, Bachelor of Theology, who writes on the book's important influence on Luther and on subsequent generations of Lutheran theologians. The 1531 Augsburg edition that I used shows three provenances, with the last ownership entry by a Magister Johann Joachim Prickler bearing the year 1684. This particular work is in Beinecke Rare Books Library, Yale University (Mck 50 530mc).

[35]The most comprehensive source for the study of the expulsion of Jews, prior to the completion of the *Germania Judaica*, is the multi-volume reference work *Deutsches Städtebuch,* edited by Erich Keyser and later with the collaboration of Heinz Stoob. Articles on individual cities are written by archivists, who provide information of varying reliability on the history of Jews in their home towns. Although there are some omissions, this is on the whole a reliable reference guide. See *Deutsches Städebuch: Handbuch städtischer Geschichte,* eds. Erich Keyser and Heinz Stoob. 5 vols. in 9 books (Stuttgart: Kohlhammer, 1939-74). For a purely economic and political interpretation of the motives for expulsion, see Markus J. Wenninger. *Man bedarf keiner Juden mehr: Ursachen und Hintergründe ihrer Vertreibung aus den deutschen Reichsstädten im 15. Jahrhundert* (Cologne: Böhlau, 1981), esp. 54-199.

[36]Stadtarchiv Nürnberg, repertorium B14/V no. 2, four volumes of register of the *Schuldverbriefungsbücher* of the city court between 1484 and 1498. These are alphabetically entered according to the legal parties involved, and a brief description of the case is noted as well. For secondary literature on the expulsion of the Nürnberg Jews, see Philip N. Bebb, "Jewish Policy in Sixteenth Century Nürnberg," *Occasional Papers of the American Society for Reformation Research* (1977): 125-36.

The impact of the Reformation on the intellectual world of the elites helped to undermine the magical notions behind ritual murder discourse. Two other developments in the first half of the sixteenth century also played a crucial role: the Emperor Charles V explicitly condemned ritual murder trials in 1544, and the Jews themselves were better organized for their own legal defense. I will give an example to illustrate this transformation, in which legality, not magic, now became the determining factor in blood libel discourse. In 1563, a leathermaker journeyman in Worms went before the city council and reported that he saw the Jew Abraham carrying a Christian infant under his overcoat into the Jewish quarter.[37] The magistrates held both Abraham and the journeyman. They interrogated Abraham on March 18, but failed to get any confession. The matter might have ended there if Abraham's relatives had not filed a lawsuit in the Reichskammergericht in Speyer, citing violation of the imperial injunction against ritual murder trials.[38] Thoroughly entangled in a lawsuit which threatened to bring imperial sanctions against the city, the magistrates dragged their feet and negotiated a face-saving solution, releasing Abraham on bail after more than a year's imprisonment.[39]

The decline of magical discourse was also manifest in the way historical documents were interpreted. Whereas the 1470 Endingen trial record provided historical "proof" of the magical crimes of the Jews when it was entered in the *Kopialbuch* of Freiburg, serving moreover as a historical reference for the 1504 Freiburg trial, a different approach to historical and legal records can be seen one century later.

On September 9, 1611, the officials of the Cologne archiepiscopal government in Arnsberg wrote to the city council of Frankfurt.[40] In the letter they reported on the arrest of several Jews who were accused of torturing and murdering a child in the town of Brilon. Further charges were brought to their attention that Frankfurt Jews had committed similar crimes. The imprisoned Jews maintained their innocence and begged the Cologne officials to write to Frankfurt so that the city fathers "might open up their old and new protocol and find out for themselves whether such stories had ever been recorded. . . ."[41] The Frankfurt magistrates spent more than a

---

[37]See Stadtarchiv Worms Judenschaft 2030. For Abraham's interrogation see fols. 1-22.

[38]On the citation by the Reichskammergericht, see StdA Wo 2030, fols. 32-33, Urkunde of March 26; and two copies, fols. 35-37. For the legal brief prepared by Abraham's lawyer in Speyer, see fols. 38-48.

[39]On the back of a letter of supplication written by Buttlin, Abraham's wife, dated September 10, 1563, urging the magistrates to quickly settle the affair, the city secretary noted the consensus of the magistrates ". . . to settle the matter as best as possible." StdA Wo, 2030, fols. 276-79. For Abraham's sworn bail document, see fols. 359-67.

[40]This letter, together with the reply of the city council of Frankfurt, is deposited in StdA Fr Ugb E47p.

[41]StdA Fr Ugb E 47p: "Sie wolten Ihre alte unndt neuwe Prothocolla aufschlagen unndt sich darauss erkundigen lassen, ob solch geschicht sich daselbst jemahls zugetragen. . . ."

month examining conciliar protocols for the last century and a half and replied on October 7. Upon investigation of their own archives, the city fathers found two cases of false charges. Other than these two incidents of 1504 and 1593, the Frankfurt magistrates reported, they could not find any more evidence in the archives. Regarding the painting on the Brückenturm, one of the watchtowers of the city known for its depiction of the ritual murder of Simon of Trent in 1474, the magistrates wrote that it did not depict a murder in Frankfurt but a murder in far away Trent many years ago. At the further request of the Frankfurt Jews, the magistrates enclosed a copy of the imperial mandate of Rudolf II (1577) confirming the privileges of the Jews and condemning ritual murder charges.[42]

In Worms and Frankfurt, suspicions and accusations escalated into official investigations but did not become condemnations and executions. In other words, the structure underlying ritual murder and host desecration discourse was undermined. Not only was the magical discourse about Jews repressed by a legal/political discourse, when imperial mandates and magisterial jurisprudence dismissed charges, but the dissolution of the tripartite structure of ritual murder discourse allowed for new and differentiated articulations of the individual components which formerly comprised a magical discourse. Thus, the disenchantment of Christianity and the dismissal of Jews as magicians did not have to result in a self-critical, self-conscious confrontation with a dubious past; rather, the single magical myth, fabricated out of diverse events in the century between 1450 and 1550, was transformed into differentiated historical "facts," and further transmitted by theological dissertations, academic studies of Jews, history books, and folk tales.

Legacy

Displaced by a new legal/political discourse, the myth of Jewish magic nevertheless got passed on into the realm of cultural and historical discourse. Myth was no longer a part of a living magical world in which ideas and events flowed in and out of a unified, reality-ordering structure; it became history. The Frankfurt magistrates who replied to the Cologne officials in 1611 that they could find no documentary evidence of ritual murders in Frankfurt were also the ones who refused a petition by the Jewish community to remove the depiction of the ritual murder at Trent on the Brückenturm two years earlier, although the Jews argued passionately how the picture aroused great hatred against them and constantly endangered their lives.[43] To the city fathers, perhaps, the ritual murder at Trent was a historical event

---

[42]Another copy of the mandate can be found in StdA Fr Ugb E 46y.

[43]StdA Fr Ugb E 46y, letter of petition by the Judischeit to the city council of Frankfurt, dated November 21, 1609. Another letter of petition was written on April 30, 1612, to which the magistrates agreed to cover the picture on the occasion of the gathering of the electors. The picture was not destroyed until the 1760s.

which was just as real as the innocence of the Frankfurt Jews; both facts were attested to by written discourse, in the one by chronicles and pamphlets, in the other by the archival sources of the city.[44]

The legacy of ritual murder passed on in Protestant, Catholic, and Jewish memory. During the seventeenth century, when Protestant scholarship on Judaism was blossoming, Johan Andreas Eisenmenger (1654-1704), Professor of Oriental Languages at Heidelberg, affirmed the historical veracity of ritual murders. In his massive and pretentious tome, *Judaism Discovered* (1700), he recounted the history of ritual murders from the fifth century onward.[45] In addition to the many history books and theological treatises, Eisenmenger cites as authority the picture in Frankfurt under the Brückenturm which depicted the death of Simon of Trent. After giving contemporary examples of ritual murders in Poland, Eisenmenger concedes that

> one does not hear nowadays any more of these gruesome acts in Germany, except that, if I remember correctly, I had read in the newspaper some years ago that in Franconia a murdered child was found and therefore the Jews were held on suspicion. But since one has in the past dealt most stringently with the Jews wherever such things were committed, it is thus beyond doubt that they refrain from such bloodshed out of fear of punishment, although their hatred of Christians is just as great now as it might have been at any time past.[46]

He repeats the catalogue of magical beliefs surrounding blood and speculates that perhaps rabbis used Christian blood in writing down spells on amulets.[47] At the end of this section, Eisenmenger grudgingly concedes that perhaps in the past some instances of injustice were involved but that he himself was inclined to believe in a core element of truth in these charges because so

---

[44]For an example of the historical record and illustrative woodcut of the ritual murder at Trent, see Hartmann Schedel, *Liber chronicarum*, fol. 254v (Nürnberg Koberger edition) and fols. 285v-286r (Augsburg Schönsberger edition).

[45]*Entdecktes Judenthum: oder Gründlicher und Wahrhaffter Bericht, welchergestalt die verstockte Juden die Hochheilige Dreyeinigkeit . . . erschrecklicher Weise lästern und verunehren, die Heil. Mutter Christi verschmähen. . . . Dabey noch viele andere, bishero unter den Christen entweder gar nicht, oder nur zum Theil bekantgewesene Dinge und Grosse Irrthüme der Jüdischen Religion und Theologie, wie auch viel lächerliche und kurtzweilige Fabeln und andere ungereimte Sachen an den Tag kommen: Alles aus ihren eigenen . . . Büchern* (Frankfurt, 1700), 220-24.

[46]Eisenmenger, *Entdecktes Judenthum*, 224-25: "Man höret aber jetziger zeit nichts mehr von solchen grausamen thaten in Teutschland/ ausser dem das ich/ wann ich mich recht erinnere/ vor etlichen jahren inn der zeitung gelesen hab/ dass in Franckenland ein ermordtes kind seye gefunden worden/ und habe man die Juden desswegen im verdacht gehabt: dann weil mann vor diesem mit den Juden sehr scharff verfahren ist/ allwo solche dinge seind begangen worden/ so ist nicht zu zweiffelen/ sie auss furcht vor der straff/ sich nun solches blutvergiessens enthalten/ wiewohl ihr hass gegen die Christen eben so gross ist/ als er jemahls vor diesem gewesen sein mag."

[47]Ibid., 225.

many authorities had written about them and so many examples were cited. He concludes "that the Jews committed child murders mostly during Easter . . . because our savior Christ was crucified at Easter, and they did this to scorn him."[48]

From the perspective of Protestant Germany of the late seventeenth century, it seemed that Christians were finally disenchanted from Jewish magic. Deprived of their magical power, exposed as superstitious, and rendered harmless in ghettos, Jews remained nonetheless an alien, potentially dangerous element in a rejuvenated, but divided, Christian society. The academic study of Judaism and Jewish life in Protestant Germany served only in passing to dispel popular legends; for many, its chief meaning was to document and ridicule Jewish superstitions, and to celebrate the triumph of Christian faith over medieval magic, a victory achieved by the heroic struggles of the Reformation.

If books and theology kept alive the myth of Jewish magic in Lutheran Germany, popular Catholic revival rejuvenated the blood libel after the mid-seventeenth century. The writings of Matthaeus Rader (1561-1634) united sanctity and patriotism. In *Bavaria Sancta*, a four volume compilation of hagiographies and biographies of saints, monks, bishops, holy women, martyred children, pious Bavarian dukes and duchesses from the time of the conversions of the Germanic peoples to his own day, the Tyrolese Jesuit gave Bavarian self-image its distinctive blend of international Baroque Catholicism and provincial Bavarian patriotism.[49] Dedicated to Duke Maximilian I, whom Rader compared to Constantine the Great, the book equates Bavarian history with the history of Christianization, a process begun by Charlemagne and brought to perfect fruition under the Wittelsbach dukes, with the selfless dedication of the Jesuits. Saints and martyrs peopled this heroic missionary saga; and a place of honor was created for the alleged victims of ritual murder in Rader's story of Christian testimony and Catholic vitality. Engravings depict these little boy martyrs: the corporeal sensuality of pious suffering evokes Rubenesque cherubs, the image of redemptive flesh in the sensuous iconography of Baroque Catholicism.

Not only were old legends recorded, new ones were also being made in seventeenth-century Catholic Germany. The most successful example was the creation of the Judenstein legend. According to a long oral tradition, a three-year-old boy, Andreas Oxner, was kidnapped and killed by traveling merchants in 1462. After the infamous Trent ritual murder trial of 1475, the legend added new details: the traveling merchants became Jews, the

---

[48]Ibid., 227, "Das aber die Juden den Kinder-mord meisterns auff Ostern begangen haben/ wird ohne zweiffel desswegen geschehen sein/ weil unser Heyland Christus auff Ostern ist/ gecreutziget worden/ zu dessen verachtung sie solches thun."

[49]*Bavaria Sancta*, three parts (Munich, 1615). German translations were published in Augsburg (1714), Straubing (1840), and Munich (1861-62) under the title of *Heiliges Bayer-Land*.

murder turned into a ritual sacrifice, and the village adopted the toponym of Judenstein after the stone on which Andreas was allegedly murdered. The tradition was not committed to writing until the seventeenth century. Hippolytus Guarinoni (1571-1654), a physician in Hall, Tirol, collected oral stories from the people of Rinn that he published. In 1670 Adrian Kembter, the Abbot of Wilton, a Premonstratensian monastery, promoted pilgrimages to Judenstein. In 1754 Pope Benedict XIV officially recognized Andreas of Rinn as a blessed martyr.[50]

For the Jews, too, the blood libel provided a powerful motif in storytelling. They too would create a myth of magical tales. In the first half of the eighteenth century, Polish Jews were threatened by a wave of blood accusations. For the East European Jewry, it was also a time of growing fascination with mysticism and the occult.[51] Many supernatural tales which extolled the power of cabalistic magic centered on a real historical figure, the Great Rabbi Loew of Prague.

According to an eighteenth-century family chronicle, the Great Rabbi was born in 1512 in Worms. The first of many supernatural stories about Rabbi Loew appeared in 1709.[52] The most fascinating figure in these legends was the Golem, an artificial man created by cabalistic magic, using hidden formulae and secret knowledge of the ineffable name of God, the *Schem* or the Tetragrammaton.

Already the birth of the Great Rabbi portended luck and charm for his people, according to the first of these thirty-three legends: the occasion of his difficult birth foiled an attempt to smuggle a dead child into the ghetto of Worms.[53] When Loew became the chief rabbi in Prague, he was disturbed by the many blood libels against his people. A divine message was given to Rabbi Loew in a dream, and using the ineffable name of God, he created the Golem out of a lump of earth, just as God had created Adam in the beginning. The Golem, disguised as one of his many household servants, was often made invisible by amulets prepared by the rabbi and would wander the streets of the ghetto at night to catch Jew-haters trying to implant false evidence of ritual murders. When the "last" ritual murder case was exposed in 1589, the Great Rabbi turned the Golem back into a lump of clay. In the

---

[50]See the report by Cardinal Lorenzo Ganganelli (later Pope Clement XIV) on ritual murder (1759), in Cecil Roth, ed., *The Ritual Murder Libel and the Jews: The Report by Cardinal Lorenzo Ganganelli (Pope Clement XIV)* (London: Woburn Press, 1934), original Italian text with English translation, 53-55.

[51]Gershom Scholem, *Major Trends in Jewish Mysticism,* 3d ed. (New York: Schocken Books, 1971), 321ff.

[52]Bedrich Thieberger, *The Great Rabbi Loew of Prague* (London: East and West Library, 1955), 8-9, 20-22. The tales were first collected and published by Jüdel Rosenberg in 1909 under the title of *Niphloath ha-Maharal,* with a German translation by Chaim Bloch.

[53]Chayim Bloch, *The Golem: Legends of the Ghetto of Prague,* trans. Harry Schneiderman (Vienna: The Golem, 1925), Fourth Story.

fantasy world of these cabalistic legends, the prophylactic function of the sacred word was extended to protect Jews against the blood libel. In the Jewish discourse on ritual murder, Word magic served as the charm to ward off Blood magic.

¶ The ende and last confession of mother Waterhouse at her death, whiche was the xxix. daye of July.

Anno. 1 5 6 6.

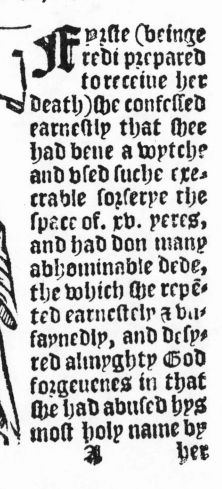

Mother Waterhouse.

IF criste (beinge redi prepared to receiue her death) she confessed earnestly that shee had bene a wytche and vsed suche execrable sorserye the space of. xv. yeres, and had don many abhominable dede, the which she repēted earnestely & vnfaynedly, and desyred almyghty God forgeuenes in that she had abused hys most holy name by

I   her

The ende and last confession of mother Waterhouse at her death, whiche was the xxix daye of July Anno 1566

The Devil and the German People: Reflections on the Popularity of Demon Possession in Sixteenth-Century Germany

H. C. Erik Midelfort

ON PALM SUNDAY OF 1574, Judith Klatten, a girl from the Neumark (Brandenburg) village of Helpe, took the holy sacrament as was her wont, but instead of feeling spiritually nourished that day, she felt a cold wind rushing around her.[1] Later that same Sunday she passed out and was carefully laid in her bed, fully clothed. The coma-like trance into which she fell lasted for weeks, and months, and finally for almost five years. What made her condition even more remarkable was that to all appearances for all this time she ate and drank nothing, and consequently excreted nothing. This supernatural fast roused the suspicions of even her own father, who reportedly spied on her to see if she was secretly getting up to take nourishment, but he saw nothing. For five years Judith Klatten hardly spoke, except to respond *ja* or *nein* when she was questioned. And for years apparently she attracted little attention beyond her village. But in the fifth year of her strange condition, in 1578, the Lutheran pastor Caspar Gloxinus came out from town to visit her, thinking that she might perhaps be possessed by the Devil. But this suspicion, too, was shattered by the fact that now the girl prayed properly and confessed her sins. Even so she still refused food, and Pastor Gloxinus, now suspecting fraud, urged that she be brought into town. And so on August 2, 1578, Judith Klatten was brought the four miles into Arnswalde and placed in the local "hospital" (or nursing home) where she was to be observed day and night.

Under these new conditions she held out only four days before she admitted that she was hungry. After consuming a wine soup with relish she told her attendant that over the past five years she had indeed eaten, but not in any normal fashion:

> Little tiny men and maids wearing beautiful ornaments (whom she alone of all the family could see) ran about every day under her bed and brought her food from whatever was being cooked at home or roasted elsewhere.[2]

---

[1] My account depends on Andreas Angelus, *Wider Natur und Wunderbuch: Darin so wol in gemein von Wunderwercken dess Himmels, Lufffts, Wassers und Erden, als insonderheit von allen widernaturlichen wunderlichen Geschichten grössern theils Europae, fürnemlich der Churfürstlichen Brandenburgischen Marck, vom Jahr 490. biss auff 1597. ablauffendes Jahr beschehen gehandelt wird* (Frankfurt a/M., 1597), 206-9.

[2] Ibid., 208: "aber kleine Mänlein und Jungfräwlein, schön Geschmucket, welche keiner im Hause denn sie allein gesehen, weren alle Tage unter dem Bette her auff gangen, und hetten ihr Speise gebracht von allem was sonst im Hause Gekocht oder anderswo gebraten worden."

99

Judith had been sustained over the years by the Little People, but they were not simply her benefactors.

> They would have gladly carried her away except that someone dressed in yellow forbade it. Even so they pressed her hard and hurt her in the side and pushed her eyes shut so that she couldn't see how their eyes turned brown.[3]

The pixies or elves helped maintain the appearance of a miraculous fast by secretly carrying off her excreta in a blue-white basin. But in the end their powers turned out to have limits:

> For when they were feeding her for the last time before she was brought into the city, they said amongst themselves that if she stayed on in the village they would gladly bring her food, but they couldn't transport food to her over land.[4]

After making these revelations, Judith resumed eating a little; she now spoke a little and was able to walk, albeit with a limp. Her only fear now was that she might be left at home alone.

There may well be psychohistorians who would undertake to explain what Judith Klatten's visions of the little people may tell us of her mental illness, but for myself I am more interested in what her visions tell us about her culture. Certainly by the 1570s, for example, we know that Germany was experiencing a host of miraculous or fraudulent fasts,[5] examples of the way God gives strength to his chosen faithful or of the way the Devil, in league often enough with crafty and malicious priests, deceives the naive and plunges the innocent into superstition. Among Protestants the latter, diabolical view of the matter had come to prevail, and so it is not surprising that both Judith's father and Pastor Gloxinus suspected fraud and that the pastor, initially at least, suspected demonic possession. But obviously Judith Klatten's condition was not any normal demon possession. What I find especially intriguing is her notion that the little people who sustained her over the years could not help her if she moved into town. Regardless of how we understand what was "really" happening with respect to her nutrition from 1574 to 1578, Klatten seems to have been aware that some rural spirits could not survive in the atmosphere of a town, or at least that it made for a credible story to assert that her helpers were bound to the village.

---

[3]Ibid., 208: "Hetten sie auch gerne hinweg getragen, wenns nicht einer im Gelben Kleide widerrahten. Doch hetten sie sie hart gedruckt, unnd an der seiten gelähmt, unnd ihr die Augen zugedruckt, das sie nit hette sehen müssen, wie ihr denn die Augen braun gewesen."

[4]Ibid., 209: "Item da sie sie auch zuletzt ehe sie in die Stadt gebracht gespeiset, hetten sie untereinander gesaget, Wenn sie im Dorff bliebe, wolten sie ihr wol Speise bringen, aber uber Landt Köndten sie sie nicht Speisen." The substantial town of Arnswalde lies about 30 miles north of Landsberg/Warthe and about 37 miles east of Stettin.

[5]Johan Weyer, *De lamiis liber. Item de commentitiis jejuniis* (Basel, 1577); on the general phenomenon, see Rudolph M. Bell, *Holy Anorexia* (Chicago: University of Chicago Press, 1985).

Certainly in the sixteenth century many observers agreed that some spirits were bound to particular waters, others to particular mountains or caves or mines, others still to specific crystals or houses or forests. The writings of Paracelsus, for example, abound with nymphs, sprites, kobolds, elves, dwarves, and fairies.[6] He and his followers held that nature was full of such spirits. Heinrich Kornmann, for example, published a Latin treatise in 1611, firmly based on Paracelsan principles, in which he undertook to set forth all the kinds of spirits that inhabit the fires, airs, waters, and earths of our experience, and his example must stand for many.[7] It is equally well known that the miners of Germany had a rich mythology about the *Bergmännlein* who sometimes helped and sometimes exasperated them in their subterranean labors.[8] The world of ordinary experience in the villages of sixteenth-century Germany was also full of spirits, who might frighten the cattle, spoil the beer, and keep butter from forming in the churn.

It is hard to find out much in detail about these spirits and goblins and elves because literate people usually described such ideas as superstition. For Lutherans and Catholics alike, the world was not full of all sorts of spirits. Instead there were, fundamentally, only two kinds of spirits in the world: good angels and bad; and of the two, devils were far the more active. Indeed, one of the most pervasive processes across the sixteenth century, and not just in Germany, was the growing demonization of the world. The learned and literate found that it made better sense of their world to describe the apparent

[6]Jodus Hocker, "Der Teuffel selbs," in Sigmund Feyrabend, ed., *Theatrum Diabolorum, Das ist: Warhaffte eigentliche und kurtze Beschreibung Allerley grewlicher schrecklicher und abschewlicher Laster, so in diesen letzten, schweren, und bösen Zeiten, zu allen Orten und Enden fast bräuchlich* (Frankfurt a/M., 1587), fol. 12v; Mechtild Josephi Jacob, "Die Hexenlehre des Paracelsus und ihre Bedeutung für die modernen Hexenprozesse: Ein Beitrag zur Geschichte der Entwicklung des Hexenglaubens seit dem Mittelalter unter besonderer Berücksichtigung der Überlieferung aus dem Raum Gifhorn (Braunschweig)," (Ph.D. diss., Göttingen University, 1959); Charles Webster, "Paracelsus and Demons: Science as a Synthesis of Popular Belief," in *Scienze, credenze occulte, livelli di cultura*, pub. by the Istituto Nazionale di Studi sul Rinascimento (Florence: Olschki, 1982), 3-20.

[7]Henricus Kornmann, *Templum Naturae Historicum, . . . in quo de natura et miraculis quatuor elementorum . . . disseritur* (Darmstadt, 1611); see also Allen G. Debus, *The Chemical Philosophy: Paracelsan Science and Medicine in the Sixteenth and Seventeenth Centuries*, 2 vols. (New York: Science History Publications, 1977); for a short introduction, see Lynn Thorndike, *A History of Magic and Experimental Science*, vol. 5: *The Sixteenth Century* (New York: Macmillan, 1941), 617-51.

[8]Henning Gross, *Magica. Das ist: Wunderbarliche Historien von Gespensten und mancherley Erscheinungen der Geister*, 2 vols. (Eisleben, 1600), 1: 35r-36r; Georg Schreiber, *Alpine Bergwerkskultur: Bergleute zwischen Graubünden und Tirol in den letzten vier Jahrhunderten* (Innsbruck: Wagner, 1956); Gerhard Heilfurth and I. M. Greverus, *Bergbau und Bergmann in der deutschsprachigen Sagenüberlieferung Mitteleuropas*, vol. 1 (Marburg: Elwert, 1967); P. Wolfersdorf, "Die dämonischen Gestalten der schwäbischen Volksüberlieferung" (Ph.D. diss., Tübingen, 1949). Most of the older literature is cited in the entry "Berggeister," in E. Hoffmann-Krayer and Hans Bächtold-Stäubli, eds., *Handwörterbuch des deutschen Aberglaubens* (Berlin: De Gruyter, 1927-42), vol. 1: cols. 1071-83.

chaos of life as a dramatic encounter of good with evil, of angelic with diabolical.

The process of demonization has been particularly well studied in the area of Lutheran ethics, for here the process resulted in an entirely new genre of literature, the *Teufelbücher*, in which all the old vices of vanity, drunkenness, gluttony, lust, gambling, and infidelity were transformed.[9] What Sebastian Brant and his generation around 1500 had attributed to folly in the *Ship of Fools* and in the *Narrenliteratur* that sprang from Brant's inspired model was rebaptized and reinterpreted as diabolic, starting in the 1550s with such works as Görlitz's *Sauffteufel* and Musculus's *Hosenteufel, Fluchteufel,* and *Eheteufel*.[10] By the 1560s the genre had become a publishing fad, with as many as twenty-one "devils" detected and described by (mainly) Gnesio-Lutheran moralists up to 1569. The odd result of this flurry was not exactly what the authors earnestly intended. If every vice had not just some foolish blindness at its base but a specific devil, then the Devil himself could begin to seem foolish, consuming his destructive energies in the effort to tempt mankind to wear large ruffled collars, pointed shoes, pleated shirts, and enormous pantaloons, or coaxing would-be Christians into un-Christian dancing, swearing, disobedience to masters, melancholy, and general laziness.[11] It should be more widely recognized that even among the literate and learned the Devil had an amazing variety of shapes, ranging from these faintly ridiculous echoes of the medieval vice and folly figures up to figures of full apocalyptic terror. Before we draw too sharp a contrast between the Devil of the learned and the demons of the people, therefore, we should have firmly in mind the fact that even among the learned, and even during the process I have called the demonization of the world, the learned and literate were hardly unanimous in their view of what was meant when it was said that the Devil was everywhere. Even so it would be foolish to deny that popular and learned culture diverged over just such an issue, as the history of witchcraft suggests.

[9]Max Osborn, *Die Teufelliteratur des XVI. Jahrhunderts*, Acta Germanica 3.3 (Berlin: Mayer & Müller, 1893); Heinrich Grimm, "Die deutschen 'Teufelbücher' des 16. Jahrhunderts: Ihre Rolle im Buchwesen und ihre Bedeutung," in *Archiv für Geschichte des Buchwesens* 16 (1959): 1733-1790; Bernhard Ohse, *Die Teufelliteratur zwischen Brant und Luther,* (Ph.D. diss., Freie Universität Berlin, 1961); now we have a meticulously edited selection of devil books: Ria Stambaugh, ed., *Teufelbücher in Auswahl*, 5 vols. (Berlin: De Gruyter, 1970-80); and an analysis of all the Devil tales in Rainer Alsheimer, "Katalog protestantischer Teufelserzählungen," in Wolfgang Brückner, ed., *Volkserzählung und Reformation: Ein Handbuch zur Tradierung und Funktion von Erzählstoffen und Erzählliteratur im Protestantismus* (Berlin: E. Schmidt, 1974), 417-519.

[10]Barbara Könneker, *Wesen und Wandlung der Narrenidee im Zeitalter des Humanismus: Brant, Murner, Erasmus* (Wiesbaden: Steiner, 1966); Joel Lefebvre, *Les fols et la folie: Étude sur les genres du comique et la création littéraire en Allemagne pendant la Renaissance* (Paris: Klincksieck, 1968).

[11]Ohse, *Teufelliteratur*, 91-106.

In the history of witchcraft we are now familiar with the consequences of the growing demonization of the learned and literate world. The studies of Norman Cohn and Richard Kieckhefer suggested that the full European belief in witchcraft (with demonic pact, flight to the Sabbath, and sexual intercourse with the Devil) was a learned fantasy, one that had few if any roots among the supposedly ignorant villagers, whose witchcraft remained concentrated on the practical advantages to be obtained from cunning men and wise women and on the frightful damage that could be wrought through the *maleficium* of harmful witches.[12] Pushed to unacceptable extremes in the work of Robert Muchembled,[13] this model of competing conceptions of witchcraft (learned *vs.* popular) has nonetheless prompted a great deal of important work.[14] No one can be content any longer with the bland generalizations of fifteen or twenty years ago concerning the common beliefs of "everyone" or of "the people." We need to ask exactly whose beliefs we are studying.

And that brings us back to Judith Klatten. What were her beliefs about the spirits who helped her? Evidently, as a pious girl, she did not share the view that such spirits must be devils; but our source, the *Wider Natur und Wunderbuch* of Andreas Angelus (Engel), does not permit us to say much more about Klatten's understanding of what had happened to her. If we simply applied to her situation the findings of the recent witchcraft scholars, we might be tempted to suggest that the Devil in all his forms was a learned creation, and that ordinary, illiterate people lived in a different, non-diabolical world. This would be, I think, a hasty conclusion, for it would seem to rest on the assumption that if the witchcraft of popular culture was not (or was not until relatively late) diabolical, then it might follow that popular culture had no Devil. And that would be going much too far. In fact, the Devil was a frequent figure in popular speech, in slogans and epithets and aphorisms,[15] and we hear often enough that an ordinary man or woman became demon-possessed after his or her spouse invoked the Devil by way of curse.[16]

---

[12]Norman Cohn, *Europe's Inner Demons* (New York: Basic Books, 1975); Richard Kieckhefer, *European Witch-Trials: Their Foundations in Popular and Learned Culture, 1300-1500* (Berkeley: University of Calfifornia Press, 1976)

[13]Robert Muchembled, *Culture populaire et culture des élites dans la France moderne* (Paris: Flammarion, 1978). Also published in English: *Popular Culture and Elite Culture in France, 1400-1750*, trans. Lydia Cochrane (Baton Rouge: Louisiana State University Press, 1985).

[14]See the most recent work of Eva Labouvie, "Hexenspuk und Hexenabwehr: Volksmagie und volkstümlicher Hexenglaube," in Richard van Dülmen, ed., *Hexenwelten, Magie und Imagination* (Frankfurt a/M.: Fischer Taschenbuch Verlag, 1987), 49-93.

[15]Wolfgang Brückner, "Forschungsprobleme der Satanologie und Teufelserzählungen," in Brückner, ed. *Volkserzählung und Reformation*, 393-416.

[16]Andreas Celichius, *Notwendige Erinnerung Von des Sathans letzten Zornsturm, Und was es auff sich habe und bedeute, das nu zu dieser zeit so viel Menschen an Leib und Seel vom Teuffel besessen werden* (Wittenberg, 1595), fol. G2.

By studying the publicly reported cases of demon possession I hope to uncover what the ordinary people of sixteenth-century Gemany may have thought of the Devil. I have now read most of the pamphlets, broadsides, *neue Zeitungen,* wonder books, and sermons published before 1600 in which demonic actions of all sorts were reported.[17] I am prepared to claim, moreover, that certain popular views are evident in these reports and sermons, but of course such sources have their obvious weaknesses and limitations as guides to the popular mind.[18] First of all, such books make no claim to list all the cases of possession even for a given town or year. Their authors selected examples in order to illustrate a conclusion, and one can search in vain, for example, for Catholic accounts of unsuccessful exorcisms, even though we know that there must have been many unsuccessful efforts to free the victims of demonic obsession or possession. It was, moreover, never against the law to be demon-possessed, and so we cannot expect to find official registers anywhere of the possessed. Like Judith Klatten, many of the possessed may have lain in obscurity without ever coming to literate attention. We don't know how large the "dark figure" may have been.

Second, the sources I have read are often pieces of zealous polemic.[19] They can hardly be said to have even tried to present cool-headed, objective observation. When Johann Conrad Dannhauer of Strasbourg described the pitiful case of a ten-year-old daughter of a high noble family in 1654, he recorded such detailed and theologically correct conversations between the girl and the Devil that any modern reader will be drawn to the conclusion that Dannhauer himself composed these dialogues.[20] Similarly, when Tobias Seiler described the possession and liberation of a twelve-year-old Silesian girl in 1605, the Devil apparently entered into such theologically learned

---

[17]This is to be sure a bold claim, and I would eargerly extend my acquaintance to works that I have not yet considered. I know that the pious *Mirakelbücher* of various pilgrimage centers may, e.g., occasionally contain hitherto unknown accounts of demon possession, but I have read only a fraction of them.

[18]See Steven Ozment, "The Social History of the Reformation: What can we learn from Pamphlets?" in Hans-Joachim Köhler, ed. *Flugschriften als Massenmedium der Reformationszeit* (Stuttgart: Klett-Cotta, 1981), who seems to ignore some of the chief weaknesses of these sources as windows into the popular mind while proving their usefulness for other kinds of social history.

[19]This is a point made repeatedly by recent scholars. See Cécile Ernst, *Teufelaustreibungen: Die Praxis der katholischen Kirche im 16. und 17. Jahrhundert* (Bern: H. Huber, 1972); D. P. Walker, "Demonic Possession Used as Propaganda in the later Sixteenth Century," in *Scienze, credenze occulte, livelli di cultura,* 237-48; extended in his *Unclean Spirits: Possession and Exorcism in France and England in the Late Sixteenth and Early Seventeenth Centuries* (Philadelphia: University of Pennsylvania Press, 1981). See also the forthcoming study by Stuart Clark, "Witchcraft in Early Modern Thought," in which a substantial chapter, "Understanding Possession," develops this theme.

[20]Johann Conrad Dannhauer, *Scheid- und Absag- Brieff Einem ungenanten Priester auss Cöllen, auff sein Antworts-Schreiben an einen seiner vertrawten guten Freunde, über das zu Strassburg (also titulirte) vom Teuffel besessene Adeliche Jungfräwlin gegeben . . .* (Strassburg, 1654), e.g. fols. A3v, A5r-v, A6v-8v.

arguments with Seiler and with other observers, over several days, that any reader is bound to conclude that Seiler was composing not only his own lines, but the Devil's, too.[21] These are hardly examples of straight reportage. Even so, I think that we can get some real glimpses of what these girls may have actually said, some impression of how they understood their troubles, as distinguished from the theological and polemical interpretation to which they were immediately subjected. For example, Dannhauer's Strasbourg girl spoke so often and apparently so movingly of wanting to die, of being ready to die, and of seeing God, that we can surely regard her as a religiously melancholy child with strongly mystical yearnings. And Seiler's girl seems to have spoken with the voice of the Devil, threatening to leave a terrible stench and warning that he would shit in the pastor's throat to make him hoarse, a threat that prompted the attending pastor to object, "Scheis in die Helle, Gott wird uns dafür behütten."[22] Such notes, I am suggesting, have the ring of spontaneous reporting. They do not seem to me to be merely the acidulous products of overheated theological zeal although one should reckon with the possibility that Luther's scatalogical contempt for the Devil persuaded his followers to use rough talk with the Enemy. Even so I believe that Seiler was here providing a reasonably accurate account of this event. It remains true that these sources are colored lenses that distort what they permit us to see, but if we can take the shape and color of the lens into account, we may yet be able to say something of what demon possession was like to the demon-possessed and, more generally, what ordinary people in the German-speaking lands thought of the Devil.[23]

One fact on which both the learned and the illiterate would have agreed was the evident rise in demon possession in the second half of the sixteenth century. Observers at the time were so impressed with this spread of possession that no previous age, with the exception of Christ's own age, seemed to have presented so many frightful examples of the Devil's rage.[24] His attacks were a staple feature of the wonder and prodigy literature of the second half of the century. Job Fincel's *Wunderzeichen*, for example, was entirely conceived in the spirit of proving that the rising tide of monstrous births, fiery signs in the heavens, and devilish interventions in the shape of

[21]Tobias Seiler, *Daemonomania: Uberaus schreckliche Historia, von einem bessessenen zwelffjahrigen Jungfräwlein, zu Lewenberg in Schlesien* . . . (Wittenberg, 1605).

[22]Ibid., fol. C4v.

[23]I do not take the view that the literate and scholarly set of views and expectations so thoroughly "constituted" the condition of possession that any effort to get at the "facts" would be a delusive positivist effort to apprehend the "Ding an sich." I labor under no illusion that the popular view of such matters was somehow more real, and I am asking only for a reading of texts that occasionally reads between the lines.

[24]For a handy digest of several preachers and theologians who thought so, see Hocker, "Der Teuffel selbs," cap. 14, fols. 22v-26r: "Ursachen warumb der Teuffel jetzund so hefftig tobet und wütet."

storms, disasters, and demonic possessions gave proof of the imminent end of the world and the urgent need to repent so long as a few seconds remained before the end.[25] Johann Weyer's famous attack on witchcraft trials, the *De praestigiis daemonum* (1563), endorsed this point of view by claiming that in this, the old age of the world, Satan lorded it over the minds of men as never before.[26] Similarly, when a panel of pastors and theologians investigated the mass possessions at Friedeberg and Spandau in 1593-94, they concluded in their report that such demonic actions were only possible because the second *Advent Christi* was at hand. As in the days of his incarnation, now too the world swarmed with devils and with possessed persons.[27] After all, God had revealed (Revelation 20) that Satan would be turned loose exactly one thousand years after the reign of Gregory the Great: 593 + 1,000 = 1593![28] Here we do surely see the learned theological mind at work, but at its base lay the commonplace that there had never been so many possessions before. No work set forth this point of view more successfully than the sturdy treatise by the ecclesiastical superintendent of Mecklenburg, the well-known Lutheran moralist Andreas Celichius, whose *Notwendige Erinnerung Von des Sathans letzten Zornsturm* (1594, 1595) gathered all of these observations and arguments together.[29] In just the last twelve years, Celichius exclaimed, he had himself seen about thirty cases of possession, "some of whom became possessed and convulsive here, but others of whom have come wandering here from Holstein, Saxony, and Pomerania, presenting such horrible spectacles that modest souls have been thoroughly disgusted."[30] To understand such sufferings and to learn how to treat the miserably possessed were, therefore, timely, even urgent, tasks.

With the weight of so much contemporary opinion, it is perhaps odd that this phenomenon has never been studied with any care before, especially

---

[25]Job Fincel, *Wunderzeichen: Der dritte Teil, so von der zeit an, da Gottes wort in Deudschland, Rein und lauter geprediget worden, geschehen und ergangen sind* (Jena, 1562); on Fincel generally see Heinz Schilling, "Job Fincel und die Zeichen der Endzeit," in Brückner, *Volkserzählung und Reformation*, 325-92.

[26]Weyer, *De praestigiis daemonum, et incantationibus ac veneficiis Libri sex, postrema editione sexta aucti et recogniti* (Basel, 1583), col. 43.

[27]Andreas Angelus, *Annales Marchiae Brandenburgicae, das ist, Ordentliche Verzeichnus und Beschreibung der fürnemsten . . . Jahrgeschichten und Historien, so sich vom 416. Jahr vor Christi geburt, bis auffs 1596. Jahr . . . begeben . . . haben* (Frankfurt/Oder, 1598), 414-26: "Ein kurtz bedencken, was von dem betrübten zustande der bessessenen in Spandow, und von den Englischen Erscheinungen, zu halten, Auch was vor billiche und Christliche Mittel zugebrauchen sein," at p. 417.

[28]Ibid., 417; see Robin B. Barnes, *Prophecy and Gnosis: Apocalypticism in the Wake of the Lutheran Reformation* (Stanford: Stanford University Press, 1988), for a discussion of this sort of Lutheran numerology.

[29]See above, n. 16.

[30]Celichius, *Notwendige Erinnerung*, fol. B2r.

on the basis of German materials.[31] One reason for the apparent neglect has been the distinctly provincial view of certain medievalists that demon possession belongs as a topic to the medievalists. Not so long ago, for example, André Goddu came to the extraordinary conclusion that between the years 300 and 1700 exorcism was mainly "successful" in the early and high Middle Ages but that the "failure rate" rose dramatically in the period 1400 to 1700, leading to more stringent tests for true possession and a much more restricted use of exorcism.[32] The source of such conclusions is Goddu's curiously statistical reading of the *Acta Sanctorum,* a dramatically inappropriate data base for such conclusions. Apparently the *Acta* report only three exorcisms for the sixteenth century, and they were relative failures. But even the vaguest glance at the activities of the Catholics and Counter-Reformers should suffice to persuade a temperate observer that the sixteenth century was full of triumphant success stories, trumpeted boldly by proud exorcists and their supporters, who were quick to argue that the repeated Catholic successes in expelling demons pointed to the truth of the Catholic religion and the coming triumph of the Roman Church.[33] What Dr. Goddu's hasty conclusion can teach us, therefore, is the danger of becoming trapped within one kind of source, one genre, one set of assumptions. This is a real danger for my study of demon possession, too, based as it is on what was "publicly known" in the sixteenth century. Still, with the warning that my conclusions are based on heaps of mainly printed sources, I am prepared to repeat that demon possession became epidemic in Germany only after about 1560.

To illustrate the rise of demon possession I have prepared a table of the publicly known possession cases from ca. 1490 to ca. 1650 in the German-speaking lands. At least thirty-two places were touched by possession

[31]It was on the minds of nineteenth-century scholars, e.g. Gustav Freytag, "Der deutsche Teufel im 16. Jahrhundert," in his *Bilder aus der deutschen Vergangenheit,* 2 vols. (Berlin: Knaur, 1927), 2: 114-42; and Johannes Janssen, *Geschichte des deutschen Volkes seit dem Ausgang des Mittelalters,* 8 vols. (Freiburg im Breisgau: Herder, 1879-94), 6:409-508.

[32]André Goddu, "The Failure of Exorcism in the Middle Ages," in Albert Zimmermann and Gudrun Vuillemin-Diem, eds., *Soziale Ordnungen im Selbstverständnis des Mittelalters,* Miscellanea Mediaevalia, vol. 12/2 (Berlin: De Gruyter, 1980), 540-57.

[33]See Walker, "Demonic Possession Used as Propaganda" (above, n. 19); for Germany, see Martin Eisengrein, *Unser liebe Fraw zu Alten Oetting* (Ingolstadt, 1571); note the attacks of Johann Marbach, *Von Mirackeln und Wunderzeichen* (Augsburg, 1571), and of Martin Chemnitz, *Examination of the Council of Trent,* trans. Fred Kramer, 4 vols. (St.Louis: Concordia, 1971-86), 3:404, Petrus Thyraeus, *Daemoniaci, Hoc est: de obsessis a spiritibus daemoniorum hominibus liber unus* (Cologne, 1598); Martin Delrio, *Disquisitionum magicarum libri sex* (Louvain, 1599-1600); Sixtus Agricola and Georg Witmer, *Erschröckliche gantz warhafftige Geschicht welche sich mit Apolonia, Hannsen Geisslbrechts . . . Haussfrawen, so . . . von dem bösen Feind gar hart besessen. . .* (Ingolstadt, 1584); Georg Scherer, S.J., *Christliche Erinnerung Bey der Historien von jüngst beschehener Erledigung einer Junckfrawen, die mit zwölfftausent sechs hundert zwey und fünfftzig Teufel besessen gewesen.* (Ingolstadt, 1583). See also Marc Venard, "Le démon controversiste," in *La controverse religieuse (XVIe-XIXe siècles),* 2 vols. (Montpellier: Université Paul Valéry, 1980), 2: 45-60.

between 1490 and 1559, a span of seventy years; but the next twenty years (1560-79) found twenty-three places infected; and the last twenty years of the century (1580-99) added a further forty-four locations (and a generous increase in scale as well). I do not think that we should regard this apparent increase as an artifact, a product, let us say, of better publicity or better survival of the appropriate sources. If such factors were important we would have a hard time explaining the apparently dramatic drop in possession cases in the first half of the seventeenth century, a time period during which I record only fourteen publicly known cases of demon possession in the various Germanies.

Therefore we should confront the fact that demon possession cases became common in Germany just as witchcraft was generally assuming the dimensions of an epidemic as well. It is well known that Germany experienced relatively few and small witchcraft trials from ca. 1490 to 1560, but that from then on the panic began to spread.[34] Were the two sorts of diabolical activity connected? In several well-known cases the answer is definitely yes. One widespread assumption was that witches could cause another person to become demon-possessed, an assumption so widespread that already in 1563 Johann Weyer devoted book 3 of his *De praestigiis daemonum* (this became book 4 in editions of the work published in 1567 and later) to refuting it as an absurdity.[35] His critique went unattended in many cases, such as in the 1583 possession and exorcism of Anna Schlutterbäurin, whose very own grandmother was convicted and executed for causing the granddaughter's possession.[36] Dannhauer's report from 1654 of the miserably possessed girl in Strasbourg contained the same information, and although the girl could not be helped in any dramatic way, at least the witch responsible for her troubles could be eliminated, by burning.[37] Roughly speaking, this was the crime of the witches at Salem, Massachusetts, forty years later, for they, too, were convicted of bewitching the tormented girls of Salem. The problem with proving the guilt of a witch accused of causing the possession of another was that invariably the accusation lay in the mouth of one who was known to be full of the Devil, the very father of lies. From the beginning of the great witch-hunts after 1560, therefore, theologians

[34]See Gerhard Schormann, *Hexenprozesse in Deutschland* (Göttingen: Vandenhoeck & Ruprecht, 1981), and Brian P. Levack, *The Witch Hunt in Early Modern Europe* (London: Longman, 1987), 152-68.

[35]Weyer did not add a book to the *De praestigiis* in 1567, as some have carelessly thought; he merely divided book two into books two and three. For a discussion of the logic of Weyer's argumentation, see my forthcoming essay, "Johann Weyer in theologischer, medizinischer, und rechtsgeschichtlicher Hinsicht," in Otto Ulbricht, ed., "Vom Unfug des Hexenprozesses: Gegner der Hexenprozesse von Weyer bis Spee" (to be published in 1989).

[36]Georg Scherer, S. J. *Christliche Erinnerung* (above, n. 33); Peter Obermayer, "Der Wiener Hexenprozess des Jahres 1583" (Ph.D. diss, University of Vienna, 1963).

[37]Dannhauer, *Scheid- und Absag-Brieff* (above, n. 20), fol. A1r-v.

and jurists repeatedly cautioned against taking the accusations of the possessed as serious evidence.[38] And this caution *was* so widely heeded that we cannot draw any general connection between cases of possession and the rising tide of witchcraft prosecutions.

This parallel to witchcraft is worth exploring in some detail, for even if one did not regularly cause the other, there are similarities we should not overlook. For example, physicians, jurists, and theologians agreed that women were more likely to fall into the crime of witchcraft, and they cited all the well-known spiritual and physical weakness of women, especially post-menopausal women. In their weaknesses, loneliness, poverty, melancholy, infidelity, uncontrollable fantasies, and general sexual frustration, old women made easy victims for the Devil, who usually offered them comfort, riches, companionship, dances, feasts, and an active sex life.[39] So much for the general theory. The match with judicial reality was surprisingly exact. We know that roughly 80 percent of the persons executed as witches in Europe were women, and that older women were more commonly convicted than younger girls or young married women. What we have hitherto failed to notice is that the very same medical and theological reasons existed for expecting demonic possession to predominate among older women as well.[40] The Devil was keen to exploit the weakness, loneliness, infidelity, and melancholy of old women, and yet here we historians have been trained or misled, especially by a few celebrated French episodes, to think that demon possession was mainly an affair with young women, especially nuns.[41] Medical theory in the sixteenth century did regularly note the mental hazards of celibacy for cloistered nuns, but even for physicians it was old nuns who were most at risk, owing to their excessive dryness. Young women were supposedly too healthy to be regular victims of the Devil, and they constitute therefore a major breach in the link between medico-theological theory and actual cases of demon possession. If we look carefully, however, we will find an even more dramatic breach.

[38]E.g., Jodocus Hocker, "Eine Getreuwe, Wolmeynende Christliche warnung, wider die Gottlosen Teuffels beschwerer oder banner, so in diesen ortern hemrubschleichen," in Feyrabend, *Theatrum Diabolorum* (above, n. 6), fols. 135r-141v, at fol. 137r. Cf. the attitude of the theologians of Brandenburg in 1594, printed in Angelus, *Annales* (above, n.27), 414-26, at 415.

[39]There are examples of such seduction scenes in my *Witch Hunting in Southwestern Germany, 1562-1684: The Social and Intellectual Foundations* (Stanford: Stanford University Press, 1972).

[40]Seiler, *Daemonomania* (above, n. 21), fol. F1v; Girolamo Menghi, *Fustis Daemonum;* I cite the edition reprinted in *Thesaurus Exorcismorum atque Coniurationum Terribilium Potentissimorum, efficacissimorum cum practica probatissima* (Cologne, 1626), 433-616, at 448; F. Zacharias, *Thesaurus Exorcismorum,* 617-983, at 630-31; Celichius, *Notwendige Erinnerung* (above, n. 16), fol. D3r.

[41]Robert Mandrou, *Magistrats et sorciers en France au XVIIe siècle: Une analyse de psychologie historique* (Paris: Plon, 1968); Alain Lottin, *Lille, citadelle de la contre-reforme? (1598-1668)* (Dunkirk: Westhoek-Editions, 1984), 165-86; Michel de Certeau, *La possession de Loudun* (Paris: Julliard, 1970).

Table 1
Male and Female in German Cases of Possession, 1490-1650

	Individual Possessions			Mass Possessions		
Dates	Female	Male	Gender unknown	Female	Male	Mixed Genders
1490-1559	19	10	0	1	0	4
1560-1579	10	2	0	5	1	5
1580-1599	17	15	7	1	0	7
1600-1650	5	8	1	0	0	0

From an examination of Table 1 we can discover that women did indeed predominate in the relatively quiet period before 1560, although even then I have recorded four episodes of mass possession (Geel, Lemgo, Thuringia, and Mechelroda) in which the sexes were mixed (we have no clue as to the proportions within the mixture).[42] The period 1560-79 matches our common expectations most perfectly, with ten individual female cases and five cloisters compared to only two male individual cases, but even in this period there was one mass possession of boys (thirty boys from Amsterdam, 1566) and one mixed mass possession (among the citizens of Hamm). Thereafter, our expected picture runs into even more trouble. For the period 1580-99, male individual possessions ran about equal to the female cases (15 to 17), and we need to add the extraordinary mass possessions from Brandenburg and, to a lesser extent, Saxony. The reports of eyewitnesses in Brandenburg from the 1590s repeatedly stated that the Devil seized people and shook them, sending them off into seizures without respect of age or gender.[43] Some 150 were afflicted in the Neumark town of Friedeberg, and about 40 people fell under attack in Spandau, just west of Berlin. Berlin itself came under siege, as did the towns of Stendal, Tangermünde, and the Saxon town of Lindau. Unfortunately, we cannot tell the proportions of male and female in these episodes, but contemporary observers were struck by the promiscuous nature of these assaults. Although there are only a few cases after 1600, the new pattern apparently continued, with eight men and five women coming to public attention between 1600 and 1650.

I find this deviation from learned theory instructive, for it suggests that theologians, jurists, and physicians of the sixteenth century were in no position to evoke cases of demonic possession in exactly the shapes they

---

[42]For the sources of this table see my forthcoming book, "A History of Madness in Germany during the Sixteenth Century."

[43]Daniel Cramer, *Das Grosse Pomersche Kirchen Chronicon* (Stettin, 1628), 53; J.C.W. Moehsen, *Geschichte der Wissenschaften in der Mark Brandenburg, besonders der Arzneiwissenschaft*, vol. 1 (Berlin: Decker, 1781): 500-2.

dictated or expected. Unlike witchcraft, it was no crime to be possessed, and perhaps this simple difference left possession more in the hands and minds of ordinary people than the crime of witchcraft, which was after all defined, prosecuted, and routinized by the literate magisterial classes of Europe. This means in turn that the actual cases of demonic possession, as we find them in the accounts of publicists of the sixteenth century, were certainly in part, and in some cases in large part, the product of popular fears, fancies, and images of the Devil or of other spirits. Like Judith Klatten's little people, some of the aspects of demon possession as it actually occurred were thoroughly strange to the biblical, classical, or medical minds of the literate.

Let us pursue this question further by looking at the preconditions of possession, as they were commonly understood. Throughout the sixteenth century it was widely conceded that the Devil might possess both the greatest of sinners and the least sinful of all. In order to display his majesty, God might allow a demonic possession only to show how strong the Christian sacraments and sacramentals were.[44] Or of course God could permit a horrible invasion of demons to punish the sins either of the possessed or of another person. Possession could chasten or test the faithful or simply present the power of the Devil, a display often thought necessary in the sixteenth century when pastors thought their congregations full of Sadducees, Epicureans, and self-satisfied worldlings, who refused to recognize the reality of the spirit world.[45] Despite the wide range of options open as victims of the Devil, I have the impression that most theologians in the first half of the century were likely to think of possession as a punishment for the sins of the victim. The theological lexicographer Johannes Altenstaig was content to rattle off four reasons for demonic possession: for the glory of God, for the punishment of sin, for the correction of the sinner, or for our own instruction.[46] Johann Staupitz simplified this schedule more dramatically in a book on predestination published in 1517: "Obsessio a daemone est poena a deo inflicta horribilis . . . ."[47] And Martin Luther usually thought of demon

---

[44]Thyraeus, *Daemoniaci* (above, n. 33), 77.

[45]The notion was commonplace; see, e.g., Jacob Heerbrand, *Ein Predig Vom Straal* (Tübingen, 1579), fol. 2r-v; Angelus, *Wider Natur und Wunderbuch* (above, n. 1), 79-80; Jacob Coler, *Eigentlicher Bericht, Von den seltzamen . . . Wunderwercken . . . so sich newlicher Zeit in der Marck Brandenburg zugetragen. . .* (Erfurt, 1595), fols. B3v-D2v.

[46]Johannes Altenstaig, *Vocabularia theologiae* (Hagenau, 1517), s.v. Obsessio: "Permittit autem deus . . . sive ad gloriam suae ostensionem in potestativa eorum eiectione, sive ad peccati correctionem, sive ad nostram eruditionem."

[47]Johann von Staupitz, *Libellus de exsecutione aeternae praedestinationis* (1517), ed. Lothar Graf zu Dohna and Richard Wetzel, Spätmittelalter und Reformation, ed. Heiko A. Oberman, vol. 14 (Berlin: De Gruyter, 1979), cap. 20, paragraph 183, pp. 244-47.

possession as a punishment for, or an instantiation of, sin.[48] Later in the century the learned personal physician to the Elector Palatine, Johann Lang, was even willing to opine that true piety actually kept the Devil away: "pium enim hominem nec daemon malus, nec fatum tenet."[49] This was a sentiment enthusiastically endorsed by the Freiburg theologian, Jodocus Lorich, who held that the best way to secure one's health and to escape the attacks of the Devil was to fear God and lead a pious life, for the Devil flees such persons.[50]

Unfortunately for the theory that the Devil worked mainly as God's jailer and executioner, the published accounts of demonic possession show a very different Devil, one that positively preferred to attack pious young Christians. A good example is the "gruesome story" from 1559 of the godly girl from Platten, close by Joachimstal.[51] She was chaste and modest, went regularly to church, took the sacrament often, and was said to have learned the gospels by memory. Suddenly at shrovetide she was taken sick with seizures, so that her parents thought she had epilepsy. She lay helpless for four weeks, but after Easter the Devil began to speak blasphemies from her. Moreover she began to display such classic signs of possession as eyes that bugged out of her head, a tongue that would stick out a whole hand-span, and a head that was wrenched around to face backwards. After repeated tortures and extended conversations with the attending pastors, the Devil was finally driven out through the congregational prayer and song of some one thousand common people. Before he left, however, he claimed that God had sent him to plague Anna's body (but not her soul) in order to warn

---

[48]This topic is far too complex to be passed over in a sentence. Perhaps Luther was so persuaded that the Devil *spiritually* possessed every unregenerate person, inspiring him or her to sinful thoughts and deeds, that he transferred this prejudice to those cases of *physical* possession that he dealt with. In practice with real people, however, Luther could act sympathetically and without this prejudice. The subject is worth careful consideration, but see, e.g. *WA BR* nr. 3057, Luther to Andreas Ebert (August 5, 1536), 7: 489-90; nr. 3398, Luther to Wenzeslaus Link (October 26, 1539), 3: 579-80; nr. 3509, Luther to his wife (July 15, 1540), 9: 167-68; *WA TR* vol 3, nr. 3739, for Luther's own attempt at exorcism. Recent efforts to deal with this general topic do not concentrate on the question of demon possession; see Harmannus Obendiek, *Der Teufel bei Martin Luther* (Berlin: Furche-Verlag, 1931); Hans-Martin Barth, *Der Teufel und Jesus Christus in der Theologie Martin Luthers* (Göttingen: Vandenhoeck, & Ruprecht, 1967); Heiko A. Oberman, *Luther: Mensch zwischen Gott und Teufel* (Berlin: Severin und Siedler, 1982); Jeffrey B. Russell, *Mephistopheles: The Devil in the Modern World* (Ithaca: Cornell University Press, 1986).

[49]Johann Lang, *Epistolarum Medicinalium Volumen Tripartitum* (Frankfurt a/M., 1589), Lib. 3, p. 716.

[50]Jodocus Lorich, *Aberglaub. Das ist, kurtzlicher bericht, Von Verbottenen Segen, Artzneyen, Künsten, vermeinten und anderen spöttlichen beredungen . . . von newen ubersehen und gemehrt* (Freiburg, 1593), 113.

[51]*Eine Grawsame erschreckliche und wunderbarliche Geschicht oder Newe Zeitung, welche warhaftig geschehen ist, in diesem MDLIX. Jar, zur Platten . . . Alda hat ein Schmid eine Tochter die ist vom bösen Feind dem Teufel eingenommen und besessen* (Wittenberg, 1559). This report was also printed at Nuremberg in the same year and was repeated in Fincel's *Wunderzeichen* (Jena, 1562), fols. O7r-P5r.

people to give up their godless pride, gluttony, and drunkenness. And as he flew out the window like a swarm of flies he was reported to say, "Alle die nicht gern zu Kirchen gehen, wollen selbst daheimen lesen, zum Sacrament nicht gehen, in Fressen, Sauffen, und Wucher liegen, sind alle mein, mit Leib and Seel."[52] So here was another reason for possession, one that the pastors and theologians had not dreamed of: this devil allowed a simple smith's daughter to take up the position of the authors of the Teufelbücher, to preach virtue while at the same time giving vent to her most blasphemous and irreverent ideas. It is possible that these words and indeed the whole account were corrupted by our pastoral reporter, but I think it more likely that this girl *was* pious and *did* say something of the sort.

Hers was not an isolated case. When Veronica Steiner was seized by the Devil in 1574, in the castle Starnberg in Lower Austria, she too possessed two voices, one the deep, coarse, manly voice of the Devil, and the other her own tender, reasonable, modest, Christian voice.[53] With her own voice she prayed, praised God, admonished others to pray, sighed over her own sins, and accepted the Catholic faith. But with her devilish voice she cursed and barked, spat against the Catholic religion and its adherents, and sang unchaste drinking songs and perverted Psalms. She too seems to have found in demon possession a way of expressing the two violently contradictory ways she felt about religion.

Or take the case of the eighteen-year-old maid from Meissen, who fell down in fits in 1560, but on recovery would launch into extraordinary prophecies.[54] God had been good to everyone, she reminded her listeners, but no one showed a proper thankfulness and so God's punishment was coming. Girls must give up their vanity, married persons their adultery. Woe to the rich who did not help the poor; woe to parents who did not discipline their children; and woe to all Germany for constant drunkenness, gluttony, pride, and the deliberate ignoring of godly sermons. This girl fell repeatedly into trances in which she saw God, angels, and hell. Suspicious of this behavior, Hieronymus Weller (the well-known student of Luther) examined her and had to admit that "it is nothing but Scripture that I heard, and a serious sermon of repentance, which should move us as directly as if it were a good angel's voice."[55] Here was a girl who would certainly have been

---

[52]*Eine Grawsame . . . Geschicht* (previous n.) as quoted in Fincel, *Wunderzeichen*, fol. P4v: "All who don't go gladly to church and would rather stay at home to read and don't attend the Sacrament, and wallow in gluttony, drunkenness, and usury, are all mine, body and soul."

[53]Sebastian Khueller, *Kurtze unnd warhafftige Historia, von einer Junckfrawen, wölche mit etlich unnd dreissig bösen Geistern leibhafftig besessen. . .* (Munich,1574).

[54]*Newe Zeytung, Von einem Megdlein das entzuckt ist gewest, und was wunderbarliche Rede es gethan hat* (Nuremberg, 1560).

[55]Ibid.: "aber es ist eitel schrifft, als ich vernommen habe, unnd ein ernste Busspredig, welche unns so vil, als eines guten Engels stimb bewegen soll, und ist eigentlich nichts anders, denn ein zeichen von Gott."

labeled demon-possessed at other times or in other places, but her piety prevailed in this case. She was allowed to preach in this odd way.

When the noble lady Kunigunde von Pilgram was seized by the Devil in 1565, one of the signs of her possession was that she wanted to pray but was forcibly restrained by the Devil.[56] Both the accounts by Melchior Neukirch of a possession case from Braunschweig in 1595-96 and that by Johann Conrad Dannhauer with respect to the noble girl from Strasbourg (1650-54) allow us to make the same point, but with even more pathos. In the Braunschweig case, Appolonia, the daughter of Heinrich Stampken, was known to all for her piety.[57] She loved her catechism, using it in her prayers both morning and night; she attended sermons eagerly, took the Lord's Supper and absolution gratefully, and was altogether too good.[58] One day she fell into weakness and depression, a debilitating combination that lasted three-quarters of a year, but then she broke out in fully demonic gestures and speech. With loving pastoral care she arrived at lucid intervals and admitted that the beginning of her troubles had been when she had heard someone curse her and wish the Devil into her. From then on she had had horrible doubts that perhaps she was not a child of God, maybe she was not of the elect. These religious doubts had prompted her depression, which in turn opened the door to the Devil. Neukirch mobilized the whole congregation of Saint Peter's and others as well, with repeated prayers and hymns that were printed up so that all of Braunschweig could pray at once for her release. Most dramatic and peculiar of all are the prayers composed by Appolonia herself, long stanzas of rhymed verse of which I give only two examples:

> Der Teuffel ubt sehr groß Gewalt
> Und plagt mich grewlich mannigfalt
> Nimpt mir all meine Glieder ein
> Reist mich, und macht mir grosse pein
> O Herr hilff mir von dieses quael
> Bewahre meinen Leib und Seel.[59]

---

[56]Karl von Weber, *Aus vier Jahrhunderten: Mitteilungen aus dem Haupt-Staatsarchiv zu Dresden,* Neue Folge, 2 vols. (Leipzig: B. Tauchnitz, 1861), 2: 309-11.

[57]Melchior Newkirch, *Andechtige Christliche gebete, wider die Teuffel in den armen besessenen leuten* (Helmstedt, 1596), fols. A2r-v.

[58]I see no reason to doubt that a girl might come to love her catechism, however offensive such a devotion might seem to a modern observer. Of course, Pastor Neukirch may have exaggerated her piety, but the result is then only a greater confusion of categories: it must have seemed ever less understandable that the Devil should pick on innocent vessels of God's grace.

[59] Ibid., fol. D2v: "The Devil uses great force / and plagues me horribly in many ways / Seizes me in all my members / Rips me and pains me greatly/ O Lord help me from this torture / Preserve my body and soul."

Gotts Sohn das Feld behalten muß
Der treib dich Teuffl auß seinem Hauß
Mach wie du kanst, Got ist mit mir
Im gringsten fürcht ich mich nicht für dir.[60]

Here was surely a girl who had taken in rather too much of the Lutheran teachings to which she had been exposed, or perhaps it would be safer to say that she experienced Luther's *Anfechtungen* but had them drawn out over months at a time.

Dannhauer's noble girl of Strasbourg (1650-54) was just ten when she fell to the Devil, but the odd thing about her condition was that while her body and her "outer and inner senses" were tortured, her mind remained clear and Christian, and she was able, apparently, to curse Satan herself and order him to leave her. She was persuaded firmly that she was a child of God, no doubts on that score, but she assured others that it would be better for the godless to experience her pangs in this world. "For they give themselves over to godless gaming, gluttony, and drinking, to whores and lovers, and forget all about God. But how will it turn out for them in the end?"[61] God will punish those who have not borne crosses in this world. She was not content to echo the sermons of the moralizers, however, for this pre-adolescent also had a strong urge to die. She went on and on, in words that Dannhauer must have put in her mouth; but the basic message may well have been hers: "I'll gladly die if Thou wilt, if it be Thy fatherly will. O dear God I thank you from the bottom of my heart that you are giving me the strength still to escape."[62] In some of her visions she saw God and his angels.[63]

Here then were demon possessions that produced revival sermons and angelic visions. These afflicted souls may have been using the cultural idiom of demon possession, but they were surely extending it well beyond what the theological wisdom of the sixteenth century had led anyone to expect. By the 1570s this was plain to observers such as Georg Walther, pastor of Halle, or even earlier to Veit Dietrich, the short-lived pastor of Nuremberg, both of whom commented on the pious, modest Christianity displayed by

---

[60]Ibid., fol. E7r: "God's Son must win the battlefield / and drive you, Devil, from his house / Do your worst for God is with me / I fear you not at all."

[61]Dannhauer, *Scheid- und Absag-Brieff* (above, n.20), fol. A4v: "dann sie ergeben sich dem gottlosen spielen, fressen, und sauffen, dem Huren und Buhlen, und vergessen Gottes. Aber wie wird es ihnen gehen?"

[62]Ibid., fol. A7v: "Ich wil gern sterben, wann du wilt, wann es dein Vätterlicher Will ist. Ach lieber Gott ich danke dir von grund meines Hertzens, dass du mir die Krafft giebst, dass ich noch so fortkommen kann."

[63]Ibid., fol. B1v.

the possessed (or at least many of them) when they were given a little respite from the assaults of the Devil.[64]

In these deviations from official expectation I think we can see what ordinary people were able to make of the cultural idiom of demon possession. In another area a sort of popular confusion arose. In high legal theory as it developed in the sixteenth century, the difference between the crime of witchcraft and the condition of demonic possession was clear. Witches were those who entered into a pact with the Devil while the possessed were those who passively, involuntarily endured the external and internal assaults of the Devil. What could be clearer?

But is it clear what happened to Anna Roschmann in 1563? At the age of twenty as she lay in her Augsburg bedroom, the evil spirit came to her and asked her to be his, "whereupon she began to act very strangely and as if she had lost her reason."[65] Soon she was showing the symptoms of full, raging possession, but we must note that it had begun with an invitation from the Devil. Or what shall we think of Anna Barbara of Stein am Rhein, whose very mother had cursed her and caused her to be possessed? Many common folk thought of her as a witch.[66] Truly confusing is the case of Hans Schmidt, a smith's apprentice from Heidingsfeld, near Würzburg. In 1589 at the age of nineteen, Schmidt fell in with bad company, and got hold of a book that contained the secrets of the magic arts. Realizing its dangers, Schmidt finally burned the book, but he suffered further temptations. Satan offered him money on one occasion and on another tempted him to hang himself, but Schmidt resisted these advances until he was finally possessed by a highly frustrated Devil.[67] Here the story began as many a witchcraft seduction tale began, but because of his powers of Christian resistance the youth was possessed. Indeed by the late sixteenth century many a suicide attempt was attributed to demon possession.

To take another example, Appolonia Geisslbrecht was confronted first, in 1583, by a devil who offered her plentiful food, drink, and dance. In this

---

[64]Georg Walther, *Krancken Büchlein. Woher alle Kranckheiten kommen, Item, warumb uns Gott damit heimsuche: Und wie man sich darinnen Christlich verhalten und in allerley anfechtungen trösten sol* (Wittenberg, 1579), fol.252r-v.

[65]*Eigentliche unnd Warhaffte vertzaichnus, was sich in disem 1563 Jar . . . zu Augspurg, mit eines armen Burgers Tochter daselbst zügetragen, wie sy vomm bösen Geist . . . bessessen, und derselbig . . . von Herrn Simon Scheibenhart . . . aussgetriben* (n.p., n.d. [1563]). I have used the copy in the Universitätsbibliothek München.

[66]*Neue Zeitung und beschreibung, Was sich mit Anna Barbara, vom Stain geboren, von kuniglichen stamb . . . ist worden . . . wie sie . . . mit 9. Teuflen besessen, auch wider ledig ist worden. . .* (Konstanz, 1608), fols. A5v-6r.

[67]Johann Schnabel and Simon Marius, *Warhafftige und erschröckliche Geschicht welche sich newlicher Zeit zugetragen hat, mit einem Jungen Handtwercks und Schmidtgesellen, Hansen Schmidt genandt* (Würzburg, 1589).

case she actually accepted the Devil's offer but was then at once possessed.[68] Instead of witchcraft, this case turned confusingly into obsession. Pastor Nicolaus Blum told a similarly confusing story from his parish in Dohna. In 1602 it appears that God permitted a noble student from Prague to be possessed as punishment for the sin of "Zauberey," that is, the crime of magic for which women were being executed by the hundreds at just that time.[69] Here again it may have been the youth's resistance to Satan that made the difference but it could also have been his noble and student status. We know of other adventurous students who signed actual pacts with the Devil, for example, without having to pay the ultimate penalty for their indiscretions. So it was with the desperate twenty-five-year-old woman whom Tobias Wagner tried to help in 1643. In a deep depression and eager for money, the young man made a pact with the Devil, who then prompted him to attempt suicide. When he was saved from death by his wife, he merely fell into a deeper and more demonic melancholy.[70] Why was this case not treated as witchcraft? Perhaps because of the suicide attempt, perhaps because of the evident depression and desperation. But also perhaps because ordinary people were having trouble keeping the supposedly clear categories of witchcraft and possession clearly separate. Certainly that would seem to be the case with the famous Christoph Haizmann, the painter whose demonic possession in 1677 was studied by Sigmund Freud as an example of "diabolical neurosis."[71] Haizmann, too, had a pact with the Devil, or perhaps two pacts, but he was not treated as a witch; instead, a pilgrimage and repeated exorcisms liberated him from the Devil and from his pacts.[72]

So here too we have a cloudy area where the jurists and theologians had taught clarity. I take these cloudy areas to be indirect evidence of the independent willfulness and indocility of popular culture at certain points. We would be very wrong to think that ordinary people did not have a notion of the Devil, but my examples of pious demoniacs and of those who curiously

[68]Sixtus Agricola and Georg Witmer, *Erschröckliche gantz warhafftige Geschicht* (above, n. 33), 5-6.

[69]Nicolaus Blumius, *Historische erzehlung. Was sich mit einem fürnehmen Studenten, der von dem leidigen Teuffel zwölff Wochen besessen gewesen, verlauffen* (Leipzig, 1605), 1-3.

[70]Tobias Wagner, *Der Kohlschwartze Teuffel . . . über einem schröcklichen Fall einer Mannsperson die sich in Schwermuth dem Teuffel mit eignem Blut verschrieben. . .* (Ulm, 1643), 74-75. For the demonic temptation to suicide, see esp. Markus Schär, *Seelennöte der Untertanen: Selbstmord, Melancholie und Religion im Alten Zürich, 1500-1800* (Zurich: Chronos, 1985).

[71]Sigmund Freud, "A Seventeenth-Century Demonological Neurosis," in *The Standard Edition of the Complete Psychological Works*, ed. James Strachey, vol. 19 (London: Hogarth, 1961): 67-105; Richard Hunter and Ida Macalpine, *Schizophrenia 1677: A Psychiatric Study of an Illustrated Autobiographical Record of Demoniacal Possession* (London: W. Dawson, 1956); Gaston Vandendriessche, *The Parapraxis in the Haizmann Case of Sigmund Freud* (Louvain: Publications Universitaires, 1965).

[72]See my essay on this case, "Catholic and Lutheran Reactions to Demon Possession in the Late 17th Century: Two Case Histories," in *Daphnis* 15 (1986): 623-48.

had a pact with the Devil or dabbled in magic or were suicidal only to become possessed suggest areas of resistance to or ignorance of the official word of jurists and pastors. I would be reluctant to describe the method I am using here as a form of "higher criticism," for these pamphlets and wonder books were far from being canonical texts; but there is a certain vague similarity in that we need to develop what I would call "educated surprises" in order to imagine what may lie behind a text.

Another old approach, and one still worth using, is that of simple geography. Many things seem noteworthy on the maps I have drawn, but I find it especially significant that only thirty-nine towns and villages south of the Main River had cases of demon possession and only one of these was a true obsessional epidemic (Eichstätt).[73] In contrast, northern Germany had over sixty-five separate towns with cases of actual or suspected demon possession, and several of these episodes, especially in the northeast or northwest, were massive outbursts of daemonomania. A surprising number of these northern cases came from Lutheran Saxony and Brandenburg, a fact that may be connected to the great gnesio-Lutheran controvesy over exorcism at baptism.[74] And only a tiny number appear in the great lands of the Counter-Reformation, Bavaria and Austria. Proud as he was of the miracles performed by Our Lady of Altötting, Dr. Martin Eisengrein, writing in 1570, listed only one dispossession of demons in his almost-200-page-long treatise on that famous pilgrimage shrine.[75] Demon possession does appear now and then, but rarely, in the Bavarian and Franconian miracle books; and so it seems that southern Germany, and especially the southeast, was surprisingly lacking in demon possessions and famous exorcisms.

I do think it is important to notice the frequency of demon possessions among nunneries and among the most gnesio-Lutheran areas, for in both situations the attempt to live an ever more perfect life may have led to stronger temptations than those felt in other parts of Germany. This would help to explain the account from Brandenburg in the 1590s in which the Devil was said to have strewn coins all over the streets, but whoever picked up a coin became instantly (but not permanently) possessed.[76] Perhaps only a region where the demonic vices of greed, usury, pride, and vanity had been censured for over a generation and with increasing apocalyptic fervor could have generated such a story. And that in turn suggests that when we speak of popular ideas of the Devil, we cannot mean *only* those ideas that literate,

---

[73]This Eichstätt case from the 1490s was still evoking interest one hundred years later: Julius Freiherr von Bohlen Bohlendorff, ed., *Hausbuch des Herrn Joachim von Wedel, Auf Krempzow Schloss und Blumberg Erbgesessen* (Tübingen, 1882), 348.

[74]See Bodo Nischan, "The Exorcism Controversy and Baptism in the Late Reformation," *Sixteenth Century Journal* 18 (1987): 31-51.

[75]Eisengrein, *Unser liebe Fraw zu Alten Oetting* (above, n. 33), fol. B3v.

[76]Daniel Cramer, *Das Grosse Pomrische Kirchen Chronicon* (above, n. 43), 54.

educated poeple did not share. By the late sixteenth century the German people generally believed that demon possession was on the rise, and they may even have taken the rise as a sign of the imminent end of the world. But while accepting this learned interpretation of what they saw around them, ordinary people also knew how to shape the idiom of possession to some of their own ends.

In a collection of papers on cities and their culture, it will not escape notice that my discussion of demon possession has not concentrated mainly on cities. The Devil was equally active in towns and in the countryside. It is true that Judith Klatten's Little People were symptomatic of a rural, not an urban, view of things. The spirits and goblins of Germany had no really urban form; but perhaps the classic Devil was a townsman. Certainly his opponents were. Time and again, when a demon proved impossibly difficult, a demoniac would be brought into town because there the spiritual resources of a region were often concentrated, whether in the priests and relics of many a Catholic town or in the large congregations of Lutheran towns, whose Lutheran hymns became the Protestant substitute for exorcism. And so the history of demon possession may tell us something, after all, about cities and their culture in the Renaissance.

Witches' Sabbath. 1510 Munich

Comment on "Jewish Magic" and "The Devil and the German People"

Gerald Strauss

"POPULAR CULTURE" is the title of this section, and the job of the commentator must be to draw out of the essays presented here some implications for the study of that discipline. Popular culture history, as I understand it – and I do not write as a practitioner– tries to comprehend the ways of ordinary people from within, as it were, their own world of ideas and values. This cannot always be done without a great deal of surmise and an often highly imaginative reading of the sources; but when it *is* done, it makes quite a change from what those of us who learned our history in the old way are used to. And I think the gain has been considerable. I am thinking, in my own line of work, of a recent book by Peter Zschunke called *Alltag der einfachen Menschen* about the little Rhenish town of Oppenheim in the sixteenth, seventeenth, and eighteenth centuries. Until I read that book I never quite realized what it meant to be – to exist as – a Calvinist, a Lutheran, a Catholic (all three confessions lived together in the place) in a life of toil, struggle, uncertainty, occasional fun and happiness, more often pain and frustration.[1] What did theological abstractions such as election, merit, and sainthood mean when turned into prescriptions for coping in the world? The book tells us, as it surveys birth rates, name choices, work habits and leisure use, and a hundred other mundane concerns that had never counted for much with us as scholars, but matter enormously to each one of us as a creature.

What I have just said, and the way in which I have said it, illustrate two perhaps not altogether welcome characteristics of our approach to popular culture. First, we cannot, in making this approach, seem to rid ourselves of a sense of devolution or etiolation: we want to know what becomes of an idea or theme as it dissipates itself among the many. The former remains our conceptual starting point; the high/low opposition is built into our procedures. Secondly – and perhaps this is to compensate for the elitist presumptions built into our academic mind-set – we sentimentalize. The generous human feelings we bring to our depiction of ordinary life contrast sharply with the cold eye we cast on society's top people: lawyers, theologians, magistrates, bureaucrats, and such. Or at least so it seems to me from what reading I have done in the field.

Professor Hsia seems to have avoided this double trap in the essay he has contributed to this volume. There cannot be a practice less likely to arouse sympathy for its perpetrators than the blood libel; he is, therefore, in no danger of sentimentalizing his subject. While he goes some way toward

---

[1] Peter Zschunke, *Konfession und Alltag in Oppenheim: Beiträge zur Geschichte von Bevölkerung und Gesellschaft einer gemischtkonfessionellen Kleinstadt* . . . (Wiesbaden: F. Steiner, 1984).

explaining ritual murder accusations in terms of religious and psychological drives that are not in themselves contemptible or blameworthy, he emphatically distances himself from this particular expression of popular culture in medieval and early modern Christendom. Nor is devolution a necessary part of his explanatory scheme. Professor Hsia visualizes events unfolding in a pyramidal figure of which the massive base is filled with popular legends and folk tales. In the substratum of this collective notiondom grow the common mental, linguistic, and behavioral rules by which people think and act. Thinking and acting lead to incidents – we ascend the pyramid – and in this way to the involvement of culturally higher agents who take the material for their particular thinking and acting from a different set of non-popular (we usually say "learned" or "literate,") sources. There follows a clash of two contrary conceptual and value systems, one popular, the other elitist. The victory is carried off by the latter. It has the better weapons and knows how to aim them expertly. And it is in tune with the trends of the time, which are in large part of its own making. Professor Hsia's scheme treats popular notions as autochthonous – in this case the notions are about magic, Jews, blood, and sacrifice – although their origin remains with all investigators an open question. The point is that these notions are so anciently and so deeply rooted in the soil of folk religion that one cannot usefully speak of them in terms of reception and distortion, or devolution and etiolation.

Professor Midelfort also makes an argument for the indigenousness of popular culture ideas, in his instance, ideas about the Devil and demonic possession. The sources, he writes, problematic as they are, do give us true reports of what the victims actually said, and therefore – or so we must assume – what they really thought; in other words, how they themselves understood their condition. And these occasional glimpses of genuine folk mentality show some interesting variations from what the learned literature tells us about possession. From this we should conclude – so goes Midelfort's argument – that there existed within popular culture a substratum of Devil lore independent of ideas imposed by the learned. No doubt this is true. A glance at Stith Thompson's *Motif Index* will indicate how diffusely and diversely present the Devil was in the folklore of early modern Europe.[2] But this prevalence is not what the scholarly argument is about. At issue for the student of popular and learned cultural interactions are the formal patterns in the evidence given by afflicted persons. How does the Devil make his approach to his victims? What does he say to them? What kind of speech does he use? How does the victim react? What does she or he feel? How are these feelings expressed? It is highly likely, it seems to me, that the answers to these questions will reveal structural elements in popular behavior

[2]Stith Thompson, *Motif Index of Folk Literature . . .*, 6 vols. (Bloomington: Indiana University Press, 1955-75), G 303.

that are in close correspondence with patterns handed down from above. Have the stories been analyzed for such correspondence? Surely this is what will count in deciding whether Professor Midelfort's repertoire of possession reports transmits genuine expressions of folk mentality, or reproduces instead what is essentially a literary artifice designed at a higher social level for ulterior purposes.

I want to return later to these two points: the ulterior objective of learned writers, and the artificiality of the cases they cite. It should not be concluded from what is being said concerning the struggle between cultures that this conflict was necessarily waged on class lines. Assurances are usually given – Professor Hsia offers them and Professor Midelfort implies them – that "popular" in popular culture is not meant to refer only to members of subordinate ranks in society. Far from it. Society is a cultural universe, and all who grow up and move into their respective places in it share its assumptions and predilections. These act as a powerhouse of perceptions, motives, and expectations, ultimately threatening not only to marginalized groups such as despised Jews and defenseless old women, but, as well, to dominant factions and self-proclaimed guardians of order and reasonableness in society. Thus the assault on popular culture in the name of discipline and rationality, although this turned out to be a frustrating conflict to wage in which, as in so many wars, contempt for the enemy deceived the attackers into underestimating his strength.

Profesor Hsia's argument replicates pretty much the schema by which students of early modern popular culture have understood and described the interaction between their subject and the culture of the intellectual and political elites that dominated public life in the sixteenth and seventeenth centuries. According to this schema, an unstable mass of magic-ridden, violence-prone, essentially irrational – and therefore socially destructive as well as morally offensive – folk beliefs is undermined and eventually replaced by a less volatile and much more controllable – and therefore "rational" – system of ideas promoted by men in positions of authority as a program of cultural reconstruction. There is little agreement on what this endeavor should be called. We can call it "reform" with Burke, or "acculturation" with Muchembled, or "christianization" with Delumeau and LeGoff, or "social control," a term used by nearly everybody.[3] We can think of it as a part of the civilizing process, or view it, antagonistically, as an agenda for

---

[3]Peter Burke, *Popular Culture in Early Modern Europe* New York: Harper & Row, 1978), 207 and *passim*. Robert Muchembled, *Popular Culture and Elite Culture in France 1400-1750* (Baton Rouge: Louisiana State University Press, 1985), Part 2: "The Repression of Popular Culture," *passim*. Idem, "Lay Judges and the Acculturation of the Masses. . . ." in Kaspar von Greyerz, ed., *Religion and Society in Early Modern Europe 1500-1800* (London: German Historical Institute, 1984), 58. Jean Delumeau, *Le Catholicisme entre Luther et Voltaire* (Paris: Presses universitaires de France, 1971), 256ff. Jacques LeGoff, "The Learned and Popular Dimensions of Journeys in the Otherworld in the Middle Ages" in Steven Kaplan, ed., *Understanding Popular Culture* (Berlin:Mouton, 1984), 28, 31.

cultural subversion. Or we can, with Chartier, concentrate on the use made at various social levels of cultural models offered from above, on their "appropriation."[4] But there can be no doubt that we are observing a historical phenomenon, one that really happened as, to quote Peter Burke, "a systematic attempt by some of the educated . . . to change the attitudes and values of the rest of the population," that is to say, "to improve them," to bring them into line with the sanctioned traits of "decency, diligence, gravity, modesty, orderliness, prudence, reason, self-control, sobriety, and thrift," or, to cite a diffferent list of public virtues offered by Günther Lottes, to inculcate in the mass of the population the socially desirable traits of obedience, industry, sobriety, and parsimony.[5]

In Professor Hsia's version of this scheme, these desirable traits, and the orderly, safe society that is their anticipated product, are fostered by two particular systems of superior values. These are "true religion" in the form of evangelical Christianity (Lutheranism in his particular case); secondly, legal doctrines codified to conform to the standards of scholarly jurisprudence. Both systems present themselves as correct deductions from godly and natural first principles. Both have the status of norms. Both transcend the relatively narrow academic categories of theology and law to embrace the visions of world views. In other words, they are ways of seeing things whole, which is why Professor Hsia calls them "discourses." In their own times, these two idea-and-value systems were perceived by many as juggernauts; and, indeed, they did set out to crush what stood in their way. Considering only Professor Hsia's example of this destructive mission, the victim deserves no laments. Good riddance, we say. But not all targets of the evangelical/legal complex were quite so expendable. Some of them may be worthy of a little more sympathy. That, however, is another story.

What interests me here is a problem I have with the mechanics of the transformation Professor Hsia describes in the last part of his paper, where he speaks of the "undermining of the elements of belief," of the "gradual change in the mentality of the elite," and of the "disenchantment of Christianity" – all these brought on, or at least given fresh impetus by, the events of the Reformation. To my taste, the explanation he offers is too disembodied. It floats above the human surface where real interests contend, and power is at the heart of every conflict. I do not doubt that the culture of magic declined, and with it the incidence of ritual murder charges. Nor would I dispute the dissolution of the traditional boundaries between the holy and the profane, with attendant consequences for the surfacing of accusations of host violations and similar outrages. But can this have been

---

[4]Roger Chartier, "Culture as Appropriation: Popular Cultural Uses in Early Modern France," in Kaplan, ed. *Understanding Popular Culture,* 229-53.

[5]Burke, *Popular Culture,* 207, 213. Günther Lottes, "Popular Culture and the Early Modern State in 16th-Century Germany" in Kaplan, ed., *Understanding Popular Culture,* 173.

the work of "changes in mentality," as he suggests, of an "intellectual revolution"? Professor Heiko Oberman has recently advised historians not to over-react to the former dominance of free-floating guiding ideas by attributing everything instead to the causal power of structural processes. In this case, however, we are on safe historical ground, I think, when we look for process, and when we try to discover it among the institutions and transactions of society. Reformation authorities did not depend on the force of ideas to make good their objectives, much as they believed in and were committed to these ideas. Magic *was* a threat to them. It seemed all-pervasive in its diffusion, and there was a tendency to see magic everywhere. To gain some control over this situation, they undertook a systematic effort to compel the public to accept their discipline. This effort was waged on many fronts and by many agents. Not only church and state officials were involved, but also universities, lawyers, and publicists. The Reformation, in its political articulation, created unprecedented opportunities for translating this program into action, and those who had been placed in a position to act participated with dedication and energy.

I want to offer two illustrations of this effort by the Reformation leadership in Germany to gain some control over the magic subculture. My point in citing them is that these examples show us not only the dedication and energy going into this endeavor but also the ambiguities and impediments that are intrinsic to it. The first of my examples is altogether obscure, more obscure even than Professor Midelfort's possession cases. It is an incident involving Jews and secret arts and incantations that briefly occupied the Saxon authorities in the year 1567. The other has had broader repercussions: the publication of the notorious Faust book, the *Historia von Dr. Johann Fausten,* in Frankfurt, in 1587. The Faust book illustrates the publicistic attack on the magic problem. The little Saxon episode draws our attention to the machinery put into place for detecting, investigating, and prosecuting offenders.

In March of 1567 a search by a local Saxon official of baggage belonging to two Jewish travelers turned up a suspicious looking thirty-page booklet containing strange-sounding formulas, garbled prayers, invocations of the name of Jesus, and a profusion of crosses.[6] The pair had appeared a month earlier in Pirna, a town on the Elbe east of Dresden, where their activity aroused the suspicions of the municipal council. Having found lodging in the town – so the councillors reported to the court in Dresden – the Jews approached a local blacksmith who had just hired a journeyman rumored to be *kunstreich* (which could mean clever with his hands or versed in secret arts) and bade him make from their own designs a catapult for hurling explosives and two air guns. When questioned, the Jews denied everything, but several inconsistencies in their story persuaded the council to have the

[6] I have published a translation of this pamphlet in *Folklore Forum* 14 no. 2 (1981): 69-83.

Jews arrested. The Elector's chancellery shared these misgivings and ordered the Jews brought to the capital for further questioning. The late 1560s were a disturbed time in Saxony, and the Elector August had decreed extraordinary vigilance against the movements of troublemakers. The Pirna council had therefore acted on standing instructions to keep an eye on every traveler ferried across the Elbe. All relevant facts were now carefully established. The blacksmith and his assistant were questioned and the Jews searched on suspicion of preparing to practice (*prakticiren*) against the Elector and other rulers. In the course of this search, the pamphlet containing the "conjury" was found in a saddlebag belonging to one of them, Solomon of Posen. He testified that the document came from a baptized Jewess of Prague and that he, Solomon, with his companion Aaron of Prague, had recently presented a copy of it to Archduke Ferdinand "to whom they had taught other arts as well." When asked whether he believed in the force of the conjury, Solomon answered that "he does not know what powers the name of Jesus has, for on this point the Christian and Jewish religions disagree."

The examining officials now applied for legal instructions to the Superior Court at Wittenberg, all in accordance with established procedures. Kept in prison under a technicality (they had failed to pay the required escort toll for Jews), they were questioned intensively. Both said they were schoolmasters in Prague. In Prague, Solomon said, the news of their "arts" had reached the Archduke, who had summoned them to his court. Twice Solomon had been alone with him and received a present of 100 Gulden in return for instructions "in several arts." They had gone to Saxony intending to teach "the art" to the Elector. When pressed on the nature of this "art," they stated only that they had learned it "partly from books, partly from reflecting deeply on things, and partly they had got it for money." They provided a list of things they could do, but unfortunately this document is missing from the record.

As for "the German booklet with the many crosses and *Beschwörungen*," they said that they had obtained it from the husband of a baptized Jewess in Prague but denied having tried to work the charm. Did they believe in it? On this they were evasive: "They say that they don't know for sure. When you have such a thing in your possession you try it out. If it helps, it helps; if it doesn't, it doesn't." One or two matters remained unaccounted for: a walk early one morning in the fields beyond Pirna, and a suspicious "blessing" gesture made by scooping up water in the hand and casting it backwards over the head.

Our record breaks off there. The case of the "Zwei in Pirna gefangene verdächtige Juden und das bei denselben gefundene Zauberbüchlein" was submitted to the Elector for disposition. He studied the protocol. He instructed the blacksmith's assistant in Pirna to complete the catapult and air guns according to the Jews' designs. We know that he read the "conjuring booklet," for a secretary's marginal note informs us that "Our most gracious lord, the Elector, has kept the little book in his own possession." It would be interesting to know what the Elector did with it.

The little event, which does not seem to have ended unhappily, tells us a good deal about the way in which Reformation authorities in Germany interacted with popular culture. In Saxony, as elsewhere in the Empire, secular and ecclesiastical officials, inspecting parishes in all territories and domains, gathered evidence about the incidence of magic practices among their people. Around the middle of the sixteenth century it became clear for the first time, thanks to the protocols of these inspections, just how pervasive and deeply rooted was the common dedication to occult observances which, as seen by the chancellery and the consistory, were intolerably subversive both of the true faith and the orderly society. Catholic authorities had deplored them but, mostly, condoned them. Protestants tried to root them out as a pernicious vice. They did not trust the influence of the preacher to accomplish this task. They relied on laws, institutions, and established procedures. But even in employing these, the intrinsic allure of magic subverted their best intentions, as in the case of our example. The Saxon elector tested the implements. He read the conjuring booklet. Perhaps the spells helped him. At least he did not seem to have been predisposed to deny that they might work.

The Faust book introduces us to a much more enterprising resolve to help bring an end to popular culture's addiction to magic. Its publisher, Johann Spies, was anything but a purveyor of best-sellers to the masses. In the early 1580s Spies belonged to the orthodox wing of German Lutheranism, which was at that time embroiled in a vehement battle against the followers of Melanchthon. Spies supported this conservative position by publishing, first in Heidelberg, then, after 1585, in Frankfurt, works by its leading theologians and controversialists. The rigorous brand of Lutheranism, espoused by his authors, with its polemics against Philippism and Calvinism, was evidently what Spies himself regarded as the correct position on matters of religion. Occasionally he lightened his heavy publishing program with some books of spiritual advice; but he brought out no trendy titles – except one, the *History of Dr. Johann Faustus, the World-Famous Sorcerer and Black Magician* (to quote the full title), *How He Contracted Himself to the Devil for a Certain Time, What Strange Adventures He saw and Pursued During This Time, Until in the End He received His Just Reward, Compiled and Printed, as a Dreadful Example, Ghastly Case in Point, and Faithful Warning to All the Ambitious, the Curious, and the Godless.*

When this is read in the context of the late sixteenth-century Lutheran world view, these are not the harmless phrases they seem at first sight. The Devil *is* mankind's sworn enemy. Sorcery *was,* to quote the preface, "without any doubt the greatest and most serious sin against God." Every approach to the black arts *was* a willful violation of the admonition taken from James 4, and printed on the title page, to "submit yoursleves to God. Resist the Devil."

Just how vital and timely a message this was for the still godless masses out there in the lands monitored by Lutheran clerics could be known only by someone as deeply imbued as these clerics were with the beleaguered reforming mentality of late sixteenth-century Protestantism. The Faust book was no aberration on Spies' list. It was an expression and example of his and his fellow Lutherans' assault on folk occultism, and, as such, a part of their systematic push for cultural reform.

German printers had been fighting this battle for half a century. They had issued a host of cautionary books in which – to quote the dedication of the Faust book, which is one of them – "des Teuffels Neid, Betrug und Grausamkeit gegen dem menschlichen Geschlecht" is shown to be the root cause of every ill done or suffered in the world. These so-called *Teufelsbücher* – of which it has been estimated that a quarter of a million copies were circulating in the second half of the sixteenth century[7] – are by no means the jolly entertainments they are often made out to be. Deadly serious in their objectives, they set out to brand every deviation as an act of apostasy. It has been pretty well established in the recent literature on these matters that the late sixteenth- and seventeenth-century fixation on the Devil did not originate as a popular notion deep in the grass roots of society. Instead, it was a position developed by the educated or, if we are to follow Carlo Ginzburg, shaped by them out of popular mythic material[8] – and spread by them to the populace, mostly through preaching, literature, and probably most effectively, through litigation. Without doubting that the educated believed what they professed, we can see that devilry was of great practical use to them as well. It allowed early modern opinion makers to brand every infraction as, literally, devilish. It facilitated social control and strengthened authorities in their endeavor to bring people into line with the abstract, written, urban, civilized, academic, legal, and theological norms of the great tradition. This, I believe, was the real objective of the Faust book. Its message was that all magic is of the Devil. The least bit of conjuring branded its practitioner as a partisan of Satan. Through the demonstration of this truth, author and publisher hoped to promote reform by first radicalizing, and then suppressing, the manifestations of unchurchly occultism in the populace. We do not know exactly how successful they were. But it seems likely that the book worked against itself. For its author and publisher, practicing a kind of ideological double standard, pandered to tastes of which they severely disapproved by describing in intriguing detail what on nearly every page they urged their readers to abhor. Thus the book became a crowd pleaser rather than a reform tract, and another example of the undermining of the disciplinary effort by the very abuses it sought to abolish.

[7]Keith L. Roos, *The Devil in Sixteenth-Century German Literature: The Teufelsbücher* (Bern: Herbert Lang,1972), 108-9.

[8]Carlo Ginzburg, "The Witches' Sabbat: Popular Cult or Inquisitorial Stereotype?" in Kaplan, ed., *Understanding Popular Culture*, 40.

And here I want to come back to Erik Midelfort's speculations about the discrepancies he has discovered between the stories of victims of devil possession, as reported by pastors and moralists, and the treatises of theological, legal, and medical specialists. In the latter, Professor Midelfort says, and particularly in theology, possession is always interpreted as punishment for the cyclopean vices discovered by the clerical establishment in the world of ordinary people. In the former, on the other hand, in accounts of possession told as the victims' own stories, the Devil always seeks out the most pious, most willing, and most obedient Christians. Once they are possessed, however, these paragons indulge in astonishing displays of blasphemy, obscenity, and irreverence, which leads Professor Midelfort to conclude – tentatively, to be sure – that demonic possession provided young people of serious religious disposition with a much-needed outlet for voicing their conflicted feelings about faith, church, and the pious life. In any case, he accepts the stories as genuine in many of their details, especially where they differ from the tracts of the learned experts.

I should like to offer a different interpretation. It seems fairly clear to me that in possession descriptions given by moralizing writers such as Neukirch, Dannhauer, Blum, and Dietrich – descriptions in which young victims, when they are not barking like dogs or cursing like draymen, are made to sound like preachers and catechists – what we actually have are examples of a developed literary device, the use of which, I have suggested, involves an ideological double standard.[9] Verbatim reports of devilish utterances make spellbinding reading. They are sure attention getters. And this matters: for audiences must be created and held. More important even: vivid descriptions of raving victims of possession produce a cast of spokespersons able to hold forth with an authority altogether unattainable to their clerical creators. Freshly surfaced from the depths of degradation, victims could speak terrifyingly about the road down to hell and persuasively about the way up to sanctity. Like the bemedalled Viet Nam veteran leading a peace march, or the ravaged ex-addict lecturing youngsters on how to say no, they have been through it, and the experience of having been through it made their witness unassailable. When Anna of Platten raved that all who fail to attend church regularly are the Devil's, or when Appolonia Stamken, who loved her catechism (a claim that immediately made me suspect her of being a clergyman's invention), described what it felt like to have Satan inhabit her body, people paid attention. In letting these witnesses make their arguments for them, the moralists not only gained powerful mouthpieces for their calls to piety and discipline, but also deployed the irresistible blandishment of satanic revelations, so as to capture the ears of the crowd. It seems to me that these stories – at least in the form in which we have

---

[9]I take this term from Frederic Jameson, "The Great American Hunter, or, Ideological Content in the Novel," *College English* 34:2 (1972): 182.

them – must have been literary artifacts employing the apparently foolproof method of censorious titillation, with which authors seek to warn their readers even as they lure them.

I suspect that this method, like the Faust book, ultimately worked against itself. In the end, however, despite all the many failures and merely partial successes, magic thinking *was* overcome, as the legal-political and evangelical-Christian and, later, the scientific-technical discourses made their way through the populace. I would suggest, however, that the victory of these discourses, when it came, was mainly owing to the hard work done by ruling elites in state, church, academy, and publishing house whose concrete interests these discourses defined in intellectual terms. Heiko Oberman has cautioned us recently against a too casual use of such terms as "elites," "ruling factions," and "social control." In a purely descriptive sense, he says, these terms may be valid. But when employed by social historians they are often loaded with egalitarian sentiments, and therefore prejudicial. I do not deny that this is so. We don't carry on our work without feelings, nor should we. But, as he himself points out, we have our own elites today, and, from observing them, what we learn about the behavior of such groups has bearing on our study of the past. I think social historians should hold their ground. There *were* elites in the Reformation era, and they did exercise ruling powers aiming at, or tending toward, social control. The ability of these elite groups to direct, to reform, even to reconstruct the culture of the urban and rural multitudes was vastly enhanced in the sixteenth century by their rise to unprecedented social and political eminence. I tried to show in a book about lawyers in Reformation Germany, published in 1986, how theologians, jurists, bureaucrats, and medical men were dynastically meshed in a tightly woven social network of office, property, prestige, influence, and power.[10] The social self-possession and intellectual pride of the members of this elite, and the mutual reinforcement drawn from their important positions in church, state, and the professions, made them into the sort of religious, judicial, and cultural activists for whom existing conditions are there to be changed. Having removed the detritus of folkish thinking from their own mental processes (or so they supposed), they were eager to extend this service to the rest of humanity. The extent to which they succeeded is still a wide open question. The worth of what they tried to accomplish is the real problem in the current debate about popular culture.

[10]Gerald Strauss, *Law, Resistance, and the State: The Opposition to Roman Law in Reformation Germany* (Princeton: Princeton University Press, 1986), chap. 6.

The Contributors

STEVEN E. OZMENT, organizer of the symposium and editor of this volume, was educated at Hendrix College, Drew University, and Harvard University. He taught at Yale University before becoming professor of history at Harvard in 1979. His publications include *Homo spiritualis: A Comparative Study of Johannes Tauler, Jean Gerson, and Martin Luther* • *Mysticism and Dissent: Religious Ideology and Social Protest in the Sixteenth Century* • *The Reformation in the Cities: The Appeal of Protestantism to 16th Century Germany and Switzerland* • *The Age of Reform: An Intellectual and Religious History of Late Medieval and Reformation Europe* • *When Fathers Ruled: Family Life in Reformation Europe* • and *Magdalena and Balthasar: An Intimate Portrait of Life in 16th-Century Europe.* Professor Ozment is also the editor of *Reformation Europe: A Guide to Research.*

THOMAS A. BRADY, JR., holds degrees from the University of Notre Dame, Columbia University, and the University of Chicago and has been a member of the Department of History at the University of Oregon since 1967. He was co-editor (with Heiko A. Oberman) of *Itinerarium Italicum: The Profile of the Italian Renaissance in the Mirror of its European Transformations: Dedicated to Paul Oskar Kristeller* and is author of *Ruling Class, Regime and Reformation at Strasbourg* and *Turning Swiss: Cities and Empire, 1450-1550.* He is co-translator (with H.C. Erik Midelfort) of Peter Blickle, *The Revolution of 1525.*

EDWARD W. MUIR, JR., did his undergraduate studies at the University of Utah and his M.A. and Ph.D. degrees at Rutgers University. Before joining the department of history at Louisiana State University in 1986, he taught at Stockton State College and Syracuse University. In addition to numerous articles, his publications include *Civic Ritual in Renaissance Venice* and *The Leopold von Ranke Manuscript Collection of Syracuse University: The Complete Catalogue.* He is now nearing completion of a book that continues his interest in Italian social history, "The Mad Blood Stirring: Vendetta and Factional Strife in Friuli During the Renaissance."

HEIKO A. OBERMAN received his doctorate from the University of Utrecht and served as professor at Tübingen and Harvard before becoming professor of history at the University of Arizona. Among his many books and other publications are *The Harvest of Medieval Theology: Gabriel Biel and Late Medieval Nominalism* (German translation, *Der Herbst der mittelalterlichen Theologie*) • *Forerunners of the Reformation: The Shape of Late Medieval Thought* • *Werden und Wertung der Reformation: Vom Wegestreit zum Glaubenskampf* (English translation, *Masters of the Reformation: The Emergence of a New Intellectual*

Climate in Europe) • *Wurzeln des Antisemitismus: Christenangst und Judenplage im Zeitalter von Humanismus und Reformation* (English translation, *The Roots of Anti-Semitism in the Age of Renaissance and Reformation*), • *Luther: Mensch zwischen Gott und Teufel* (English translation, *Luther: Man Between God and The Devil*) • and *The Dawn of the Reformation: Essays in Late Medieval and Early Reformation Thought.*

WILLIAM J. BOUWSMA received his A.B., A.M., and Ph.D. degrees from Harvard University and has served on the faculty of the University of Illinois at Urbana-Champaign, Harvard University, and the University of California at Berkeley. Since 1981 he has been Sather Professor of History at Berkeley. In 1978 he served as president of the American Historical Association. His major publications include *Concordia Mundi: The Career and Thought of Guillaume Postel* • *The Culture of Renaissance Humanism* • *Venice and the Defense of Republican Liberty*• and *John Calvin: A Sixteenth-Century Portrait.*

R. PO-CHIA HSIA received his undergraduate education at Swarthmore College, his M.A. from Columbia University, and his Ph.D. degree from Yale University. He was a member of the Society of Fellows at Columbia University and also taught at Cornell University before joining the department of history at the University of Massachusetts at Amherst in 1987. He has edited a collection of essays, *The German People and the Reformation,* and is author of *Society and Religion in Münster, 1535-1618* and *The Myth of Ritual Murder: Jews and Magis in Reformation Germany.*

H. C. ERIK MIDELFORT received his undergraduate and graduate degrees from Yale University and has taught at Stanford University and (since 1972) the University of Virginia. He is co-translator (with Mark U. Edwards, Jr.) of Bernd Moeller, *Imperial Cities and the Reformation* and (with Thomas A. Brady, Jr.) of Peter Blickle, *The Revolution of 1525.* He is the author of *Witch Hunting in Southwestern Germany, 1562-1684* and is currently at work on a history of madness in sixteenth-century Germany.

GERALD STRAUSS, educated at Boston University and Columbia University, taught at Phillips Exeter Academy and the University of Alabama, and since 1959 has been a member of the department of history at Indiana University. His publications include *Historian in an Age of Crisis: The Life of Johannes Aventinus* • *Nuremberg in the Sixteenth Century* • *Sixteenth Century Germany: Its Topography and Topographers* • *Luther's House of Learning: Indoctrination of the Young in the German Reformation* • and *Law, Resistance, and the State: The Opposition to Roman Law in Reformation Germany.*

Index

Index compiled by ASI member Paula Presley